7 Secrets for Beating Educator Burnout

PROVEN SOLUTIONS FOR EDUCATIONAL WELLNESS

By
Kenneth J. Smith M.Ed

7 Secrets for Beating Educator Burnout:
Proven Solutions for Educational Wellness
By
Kenneth J. Smith M.Ed
Published by Violet Life Publishing

Copyright @ 2024 Kenneth J. Smith

I-AM Possible Enterprise, LLC
P.O. Box 5161
Fairlawn, OH 44334
ISBN: 979-8-9853254-5-4

Visit www.coachjojospeaks.com for bulk orders and speaking engagements

DEDICATION

This book is dedicated to my family. I-AM the man that I-AM because of the village that has surrounded me. I want to thank Rev. Dr. Eugene Shy for introducing me to the truth about I-AM self awareness and accountability. Finally this book is dedicated to _all_ the people who decide to pour into the lives of young people using education as a tool.

TABLE OF CONTENTS

ACKNOWLEDGEMENTS

I want to shout out some people that forced me to grow as a teacher. Matthew Humphrey, Dr. Erica Glover, Nick Harris, Kelley Williams Bolar, Rebecca Butler and Kathy Jones. These people sat in the trenches with me for multiple years and we did things people said couldn't be done. You forever hold a special place in my heart.

To Tammy Monroe, my community mentor. You told me that outside the box learning to fit individual needs was coming. Now is the time!

Rochelle Brown-Hall, Merle Bennett-Buzzelli and Sonya Gordon all of you were by title above me and you never allowed a title to define your leadership. You were transformational in my life as a young educator.

To my parents: Ma yes I said Ma! You making me miss that playoff and championship game set an educational fire under me that has burned ever since. Thank you for not letting me waste my amazing potential. Bango, your hard working nature was passed on to me.

To my uncle Mitch: I proved you right! I never fit the mold of a "Dumb Athlete!"

To my wife and kids: You all allow me to grow everyday and learn to become better. I don't know everything but I-AM willing to be a lifelong learner. Thank you and I love you!

To my sister and brother: We are Master's!! If you know you know!

To Mrs. Dorothy Brown: You never gave me any answers in 12th grade English class. Your famous line "Look it up Jo-Jo" still plays in my head to this day. Thank you for pushing me and challenging me to be the best. You were the true definition of tough love!

Finally I want to shout out my grandfather Henry Smith. You weren't allowed to get an education and never learned to read. Secretly this has always been a fuel that I have used to become great. I-AM not finished yet!

LETTER TO THE READER

Who is this book for?

To get the best value from this book, you must first understand its purpose. If you are looking for a bunch of research-based theories that have been tested and tried for decades, then I suggest you put this book down immediately! On the other hand, if you know deep in your core that the education system's pre-pandemic procedures were extremely outdated and agree that change is good, then keep reading.

This book is designed to equip teachers (and other educational professionals) with tools for working "in the trenches" of education. This book focuses on steps we can take right now to create change. We will cover seven specific practices that led to increased graduation rates and reduced suspension rates for some of the "highest risk" (a phrase that is subjective) youth in Akron, Ohio.

The fact that you have read this far shows that you may be one of the change agents desperately needed to elevate the field of education. This book was written to dispel the myth that teachers are the only experts in the classroom and that, in fact, teachers and scholars should be learning with one another. It was written to help teachers understand the power of including scholars' experiences and expertise in the learning process and the mindset needed to shift to this way of thinking. Lastly, it was written to help teachers focus on the parts of education that they have control over. For many years, teachers have given large amounts of energy to the profession only to feel unsupported, hopeless, and disrespected. Now is the time to take back your power. Anticipating that teachers can prepare scholars for careers that don't even exist yet while maintaining their sanity in a field that continues to increase demands requires critical self-reflection. During the reflection process, you give yourself an opportunity to look in the mirror and analyze what is working that you can continue and what is not working that you can abandon. This will be a key practice that will be very beneficial for your mental health. It is important not to overanalyze things that you can't control. You are in your position for a reason.

MINDSET SHIFT

I chose to listen to my passion and take action. *"I knew I had to write this book when the mindset during the pandemic became business as usual!" Coach Jo-Jo*

After spending three years as a Bullying Prevention Specialist, teaching self-contained scholars with emotional disabilities as a Behavioral Intervention Specialist for ten years, and then switching to Restorative Practices coordinator, it was during my second year out of the self-contained classroom that showed me advocating for change was necessary. My second year out of the self-contained classroom was the year of COVID-19. Some of my colleagues had literally told me that they were "giving up" on their scholars because they wouldn't report to online classes. We were living in some of the most difficult times ever experienced, and systemic habits led us to focus only on scholars who were attending classes with their cameras on. I told my scholars every day how proud I was of their ability to log on to their computer and show up for class. Some school districts wanted to mandate that the scholars always turn on their cameras, knowing that many of them were living in extreme poverty. Because I believed that scholar well-being was much more important than scholar learning during a Global Pandemic, I had one-on-one conversations with my scholars, letting them know that their personal well-being was my focus. I know that may be a controversial statement, but due to my core values, many statements in this book may be taken that way. Common sense may tell you that the majority of teachers thought this same way, but because of the system of education that we always operated in, the rush to get back to "content mastery" became more of a priority. If I spent my time worrying about how others felt about my approach, I wouldn't have been able to increase graduation rates for scholars with emotional disabilities and who were previously classified as ineligible for graduation. I boast a 100% scholar-centered approach because I know that although it isn't traditional, it works. Working with scholars who are considered scary, intimidating, aggressive, not interested in learning, and have many other negative labels placed on them made me want to help all scholars realize that they too had a genius inside of them that needed to be discovered and nurtured regardless of the circumstances they had endured. Previous to my scholars' time in my classroom, they didn't attend their own Individualized Education Program (IEP) meetings and really didn't even know what they wanted from their education. That bothered me because many of them were high school scholars who had absolutely no clue about what their next steps would be after graduation. As I watched my coworkers make statements about scholars who were learning at a very non-traditional time, I would sit back and think. I would ask myself questions like what changes to instructional delivery and classroom environment will be made based on the COVID-19 face-to-face interruption? How will school be different when we return to face-to-face learning? What can I personally do to ensure that I keep a scholar-centered approach when it comes to educating our future leaders?

As you read this book, I want you to understand that without a mindset shift change will never happen. The dichotomy about this statement is the simple fact that change is the one constant thing that will happen throughout your life. Beating educator burnout isn't something that happens by attending the most expensive professional development programs in the world. It happens by daily focusing on a formula that allows you to control what you can control. You already are a superhero because you made a choice to enter the world of education. Now is the time for you to recognize your mental position in the system. You are a change agent in charge of cultivating other change agents. Change doesn't come without ruffling a few feathers, so enjoy the fruits of doing this for yourself. You'll thank yourself later because you will be a new person with a new mindset.

Here are ten takeaways that will help you get into the necessary *mindset* for taking action steps to positively reframe your outlook toward teacher burnout.

1. As a teacher, you must know that the expectations you have of your scholars are the same expectations your scholars have of you.
2. If you lead only with positional power, you are simply a boss.
3. Don't confuse an authoritative position with real leadership.
4. If you must control everything in your classroom, you *will* burn out. If you allow scholar voice to guide your outcomes, you will help groom lifelong learners.
5. If you aren't cultivating your scholars with skills to become lifelong learners, they will always be dependent on *teachers* as sole sources of information.
6. When you constantly help scholars understand the "why" behind their daily decisions, they will be able to make better informed future decisions without you.
7. If you continue to focus only on things outside of your control, you'll never be able to enjoy the thousands of personalities you encounter as an educator.
8. Burnout is less likely to occur when you have a passion for people over content. However, passion is not the soul remedy

for burnout. Passion without supportive resources, limited voice or influence can still cause burnout.

9. Scholars who are part of a classroom that is more forgiving with a deeper sense of caring tend to view their mistakes as less relevant.

10. Consequences are part of decisions. The types of consequences you use to shape and change behavior will constantly change. Don't be afraid to pivot and adjust.

PREFACE

COVID-19

March 15, 2020, is a day that none of us will ever forget! I remember leaving the school building, anticipating a small break due to COVID-19. The conversation I had with my last class was to enjoy these extra couple of days off because when we get back, we have to finish the school year strong. I was in my 10th year of teaching. This year, I was teaching middle school Success Prep, a Social Emotional Learning class created for scholars who had met the criteria of being "at-risk" in the previous year because of multiple negative reports academically and socially. I was challenged with creating my own curriculum for the course, and this was a task that excited me. I knew that I needed to do something different and outside of the typical school curriculum. I was the type of teacher that was very nontraditional. In my class, we would do projects, play games, have deep conversations, analyze movie scenes, dissect musical lyrics, and do anything else real-world you can think of. I always felt like the learning process should include fun moments, and if a teacher doesn't include fun, scholars won't be motivated or engaged enough to learn anything.

The learning structure that scholars had to navigate during the shutdown was the furthest thing from fun. The world was literally stuck. We had never experienced a global pandemic before, and the only way that we could successfully navigate these challenges was to think differently and use different approaches. It is not necessarily a teacher's job to change what is happening in the outside world, but having the courage to make shifts and adjustments in your teaching practice is extremely important. Teachers are presented with many opportunities to be involved in bringing about necessary change to the academic system. Ultimately, teachers can welcome the change instead of passively accepting outdated practices.

This book became a reality due to the necessary changes in academic design both scholars and teachers faced that were extremely magnified during COVID-19. The overall approach to learning needed to change because teachers had more responsibility on their plates, including managing scholar mental health issues. Teachers were also tasked with handling severe behaviors that increased from months of physical lockdown. The truth is, people were looking to get back to "normal." The problem in educational institutions was that normal wasn't bringing academic success to all individuals. Life (disguised as COVID-19) provided educators with the perfect opportunity to reassess academic plans that were centuries old. However, the educational system wasn't taking advantage of the opportunity.

7 Secrets For Beating Educator Burnout: Proven Solutions For Educational Wellness will highlight how having the courage to create and maintain scholar-centered approaches can ensure educational success that includes the scholar voice.

Dr. Wayne Dyer said it best: "If you blame others for something that happens in your life, then you must wait until they change in order to get better." You deserve your change right now; the answer to beating burnout lies directly in your hands.

INTRODUCTION: BUSINESS AS USUAL

How prepared to teach did you feel when the COVID-19 pandemic first began? Personally, I feel as if not one educator could have been prepared for what teaching during the COVID-19 pandemic would involve. Along with every other profession and industry, the world of education was literally turned upside down in the blink of an eye, and a wide range of emotions was experienced by everyone involved. School districts were unsure of how to support scholars navigating new and challenging learning experiences. Principals were forced to lead educators and scholars down a path they knew nothing about. Additionally, organizational leaders were providing information from executive leadership as best as they could in efforts to maintain order and stability. Teachers had the tall task of figuring out how they would teach their curriculum, keep scholars engaged, and improve test scores along with many other tasks and responsibilities. The crazy part about all of this is once school districts felt comfortable and adjusted to functioning during the pandemic, they began to carry on with a business-as-usual mentality. The mental well-being of scholars and teachers wasn't a priority for the educational system, and that became a light bulb moment for me. I knew the only way that teachers could control their mental health was to focus heavily on the things that they can influence. *Control vs Genius* is the lens that I want you to approach reading this book with. Teacher control is the way education has operated for decades, but now facilitation appears to be in more demand. The state of genius is innate and is being developed constantly. Others have no control or impact on your state of genius because it's far too unique. However, influences from others can alter one's decisions or behaviors, which is very important for school personnel to understand. Scholars and teachers face many different forms of influence throughout the day.

I want you to release your thought of control and focus more on demonstrating influence that helps the mindset see opportunities.

Right now, we are facing a critical point in the world of education—a global teacher shortage. Due to the increasingly automated nature of education in our efforts to instruct scholars, we have encountered difficulties in attracting new individuals to join the teaching profession. Schools fill their mission and vision statements with educational buzzwords like *21st century skills* and *college and career readiness,* which are skills that are supposed to guarantee success for our scholars as they move forward. The unfortunate thing about all of this is that classroom daily experiences barely reflect this type of educational system.

Before the pandemic, an extremely high percentage of scholars went from class to class sitting in rows and listening to lectures through direct instruction, without access to consistent opportunities for creativity, involvement, or culturally responsive curriculum. According to the way teacher prep programs at institutions of higher learning are preparing teachers, consistent scholar input doesn't appear to be a highly valuable contribution to the classroom environment because teachers are viewed as the "experts" (which both are). We have the unique opportunity to push against what has always worked so that we can revolutionize the system of education. Scholars are constantly expected to follow school routines but secretly want to be saved from the industrial education system. Many teachers have pretty good scholar-teacher relationships according to education of the industrial age, but the pandemic proved that the traditional everyday routine was extremely outdated. With classrooms being predictable on the inside and life being unpredictable on the outside, it was obvious that shit was going to hit the fan soon. We just didn't know the reeking smell would come by way of COVID-19.

Now that we have weathered a global pandemic and all of the new challenges it has brought to the plate, we currently have the opportunity to create new "best practices." Are you up for the challenge? If you are currently working in an educational institution, I want you to ask yourself these questions.

- When you returned to school post-COVID, what classroom changes did you notice?
- What outdated practices did you pivot away from?
- How are you being innovative to prepare scholars for a global economy?
- How can you prioritize your mental health realistically?
- How will the lived experiences of future teachers impact the field of education?

Imagine growing up in a society where you have had access to the internet and technology your entire life. For Generation Z, the internet has always existed, and scholars have been more globally connected than any other generation. The private messages via handwritten notes that previous generations of scholars sneakily passed to their peers are being exchanged via text messages. Scholars have access to tons of information, some accurate and some inaccurate, at the very tips of their fingers at all times. However, the majority of teacher prep programs and higher educational institutions are still operating from a framework of the industrial age. How can we expect our scholars to exhibit academic growth when we won't even meet them where they are? I'm asking you to do away with your personal thoughts and norms just for a second and just think about the inflexibility we have upheld in the space of education. I want you to think about the buzzwords I spoke about earlier: *lifelong learners, 21st century learners, global experiences,* and *career readiness.* Think about those words from the perspective of the up-and-coming scholars that are walking into classrooms. What will a career look like in 2030? We must be able to admit that we really don't know what the future of the workspace and the world of education will look like (but people in education don't like to admit to unenlightenment). Once you can look in the mirror and *be honest with yourself* about this reality, you will have a better chance of experiencing success with new generations of scholars.

Do you feel you are an expert of academic content? What does that matter if your scholars don't feel as though you like them (and not a social media like)? Technology has diminished many of our human interactions that have provided healthy connections in the past. Do you believe that you have great classroom management skills but seem to be losing the battle of punitive vs non-punitive discipline? Have you included your scholars in the policies and procedures that impact their learning environment every day? The fact that you have been successful over the years does not matter to scholars. This is not meant in a disrespectful way. Scholars are coming from a new world and aren't interested in doing things the way they've always been done. Don't read those two previous statements and assume that changing old school tactics is the reason for our many struggles. Experience is telling us that failing to merge all of our great resources to create an efficient and effective learning environment is causing huge amounts of unnecessary stress, tension, and anxiety to our scholars and teachers trying to coexist.

We are in a great position to learn alongside our future leaders. It is time to drop our egos and look at this wonderful opportunity that is presented to us daily. A scholar-centered approach to teaching will serve as the new normal in the world of education. Here are some benefits that scholars and educators will experience when they decide to consistently incorporate scholar-centered approaches.

SCHOLAR BENEFITS OF A SCHOLAR-CENTERED APPROACH

- Enhanced critical thinking skills. Scholars develop the ability to analyze, evaluate, and create solutions.
- Improved collaboration. Working in diverse groups prepares scholars for the global workforce, where teamwork is an essential skill.
- Increased engagement and motivation. Scholars take ownership of their learning, leading to deeper understanding and retention of information.
- Adaptability and problem-solving. Exposure to different learning scenarios helps scholars adapt to different situations, a key skill in a rapidly changing global market.
- Technology integration. Scholar-centered classrooms find ways to integrate technology so that it becomes an additional tool that scholars can *help educators learn*.

TEACHER BENEFITS OF A SCHOLAR-CENTERED APPROACH

- Shared responsibility. Shifting some learning responsibility to the scholar reduces the pressure on teachers, allowing them to *facilitate vs direct instruction*.

- Dynamic classroom environment. Teachers can find renewed enthusiasm teaching through a nontraditional interactive style. (*Everyone Included*)
- Enhanced Teacher-Scholar relationships. This special connection will help reduce the feelings of isolation often associated with burnout. It will also help break down the barrier of teacher-scholar relationships happening just because of the titles.
- Continued professional and personal growth. Adopting new strategies and exploring new opportunities creates opportunities to be vulnerable while providing the opportunity for teachers to keep their skills fresh and relevant.
- Collaborative Learning Communities. Creating a classroom community will alleviate stress from everyone.
- Professional satisfaction. Witnessing your scholars shifting and changing is a deeply rewarding feeling that sometimes teachers can't witness directly.

Are you ready to step out of your comfort zone and be the change you want to see in the world? If your answer is yes, then you will love connecting with "The 7 Secrets of Beating Educator Burnout: Proven Solutions For Educational Wellness." Teachers are the most important professionals in the world. We must take control of the things we can control so that we can be great. Thank you. I love and believe in you all. See you in the *trenches*.

Coach Kenny "Jo-Jo" Smith

Education has always proven the need for change and adaptability. The question that we need to be asking is how does teacher preparation rooted in self-love and personal genius become the standard of excellence in education?

TEACHERS DON'T CHEAT!

TEACHING IN THE TRENCHES

How do you feel about sharing vulnerable stories that made you into the person you are today with your scholars? During my time in the classroom, our team made it a point to let the scholars know that we are human beings who have made plenty of mistakes. Scholars in schools often think that teachers and administrators never make any mistakes in life, which couldn't be further from the truth. To help break the natural tension between scholars and teachers, in our self-contained class, we introduced ourselves by sharing stories of major mistakes that were life-changing. Everyone has a story! Unfortunately, most people are comfortable sharing only their success stories.

During my junior year of college, we had just finished a basketball road trip and were headed back to campus at Miles College, a Division II HBCU in Birmingham, Alabama. It was the start of Mid-Term exams, and despite fatigue, injuries, and life as a college athlete, we had to study on the bus ride home. I was diligent about studying, maintaining a 3.2 GPA, and holding onto an academic scholarship.

My most challenging class that semester was Economics taught by Dr. Chekwa, who had high expectations. Despite feeling prepared with study cards, during the test, I encountered a section where my mind went blank. I struggled to recall the information, feeling confused, frustrated, and under pressure as the clock ticked. Sensing an opportunity during Dr. Chekwa's brief absence from the room, I attempted to use my study cards discreetly to refresh my memory. However, my attempt at cheating nearly ended my collegiate career.

Dr. Chekwa returned unexpectedly and caught me in the act. He ordered me to stand up, and as I nervously complied, the note cards fell from my lap. It was a devastating moment as he instructed me to drop his class, effectively ending my collegiate student-athlete career. I felt a mix of sadness, shame, frustration, and anger at myself, knowing I would have to confess this to my parents, who were a 12 hour drive away.

Instead of immediately seeking my advisor, I waited until after class. Fortunately, a classmate intervened on my behalf and urged me to speak to Dr. Chekwa before he made a final decision. Reluctantly, I approached Dr. Chekwa, who was visibly disappointed. I apologized sincerely, explaining that I had blanked on the section and wanted to peek at my study cards. Surprisingly, Dr. Chekwa decided not to force me to withdraw but imposed a maximum grade limit of C-. I accepted his decision gratefully, vowing such behavior would never recur. He promised to discuss the incident with my coach and athletic director, a consequence I hoped to avoid but accepted as better than expulsion.

Weeks later, I learned I had performed well on the test and could have passed without cheating. Despite this, I received a C- in the class, though I had actually earned a B+. It was a humbling experience, and I only confided in my basketball teammates, classmates, and my parents after the incident. Sharing this personal story with my students helped foster a deeper sense of belonging and understanding. People may question why I shared such a personal incident, but I always emphasized the importance of personal growth through mistakes. Although people may judge, what truly matters is the outcome. Despite my mistake, I graduated as a Who's Who Amongst America's top scholars. This incident sparked meaningful discussions with my scholars and helped connect lessons to real-life situations. Being vulnerable with my scholars allowed us to learn and grow together, setting aside our egos.

SECRET 1:
MAKE YOURSELF
HUMAN/VULNERABLE

"The greatness of humanity is not in being human,
but in being humane."
— Mahatma Gandhi.

The term "burnout" is defined as a state of physical or emotional
exhaustion (Merriam-Webster, n.d.).

The first secret in **"7 Secrets for Beating Educator Burnout"** is making yourself human, being vulnerable, and consistently sharing personal parts of your journey. This is a game changer when it comes to connecting with scholars. Humans thrive off connections with others, and in order to build trust, scholars need to see teachers as human beings. Scholars want to know that when you leave the school, you visit places like the barbershop and the grocery store, and that you care enough to attend neighborhood and community events. Scholars don't believe teachers have social lives outside of school until they see you outside. Being "outside" will look different for every educator, and there is no one-size-fits-all option. However, you can find ways to help your scholars see you through multiple lenses by making an effort to be involved in issues that are important to them. Just like your scholars love seeing you outside of school hours being a normal citizen, you should seek to see your scholars through multiple lenses as well. Think about going to see little Tim in his leadership role on his football team, or Derrick giving the praise report during church service, or young Kisha as the captain of her cheer team. Watching your scholars thrive in the life skills they possess can create opportunities to develop the comfort of vulnerability on both sides. It's rare for scholars and adults to be vulnerable with complete strangers, and until a relationship is established, you will remain strangers, regardless of roles and titles.

Scholars want to know if you've experienced failure during your younger years and how you handled adversities. They want to see you in the role of a parent or community member. When you are in your classroom, take advantage of every opportunity to share parts of your personal side. Scholars automatically see teachers as trained professionals, which you are, but before you put on the title of teacher you are a regular person, just like them.

One consistent practice that I used contributed to increased graduation rates for emotionally disabled scholars. I began the school year by highlighting my own failures. Let me be crystal clear on what this means. Tell scholars about the times you messed up. By showing vulnerability to share personal setbacks, scholars can make a connection of life being a journey full of learning opportunities. Teachers should be very strategic in this approach and understand possible next steps that are likely to show up. The scholars with emotional disabilities that were in the classrooms I taught were considered failures by most of the outside world. Those outside opinions were so strong that my colleagues felt comfortable making comments like **"how do you like teaching those kids?"**, **"I could never teach the kids in there, all day long"**, and an all-time favorite, **"Do you really like teaching that class where kids don't want to learn?"** What kind of mindset would you expect a scholar to have if for years they don't receive much positive reinforcement? If teachers were comfortable making statements like this around me, what do you think their conversations were like toward scholars when their advocates weren't around?

Unfortunately, things like the media, social construction of neighborhoods, and societal norms can control the narrative on the perception of people with different needs and abilities. The way that teachers have been socialized to view differences between scholars has been in existence for quite some time. Living my life as a Black man has caused me to also be placed in this negative light by many people who have not had a single interaction with me (but that's for another book). I looked at this possible negative as a positive opportunity to build community in school, a place that is supposed to be full of love, compassion, and support. I felt that as a teacher I always had to prove my worth with actions and do things non traditionally. There was always a sense of pressure to stand out because my every move was being scrutinized (behind my back). My life as a student-athlete has more than prepared me for dealing with the unpleasantries.

In our classroom, the practice of sharing our failures was a collaboration of colleagues and co-teachers. When you are working with scholars who are considered by others as **"scary"**, **"dumb"**, and **"unable to learn"**, you must be creative to gain their trust. I know that this is a common phrase that has been part of education since its inception; however, the trust that I'm referring to happens through intentional daily practice. Vulnerability is not a one-time thing or something that happens during the first week of school; you establish a community by creating a space for vulnerability. Word of mouth spreads fast, and by demonstrating consistent support and promoting the power of scholar voice, my team and I had scholars outside of our classes requesting to add our class to their schedules. This was because they longed for an environment where they could be vulnerable with a trusted adult inside a safe space. Fifteen years of teaching experience has proven to me that all scholars crave this experience, whether they actively seek it out or not. Scholars have encountered many life experiences that have made them distrust people. Many of these experiences were not in their control. Some of them are laughed at and ridiculed by peers for their decisions.

Knowing that scholars require a safe space to explore their feelings and emotions is why I have always asked myself reflection questions. Some examples are:

- *I wonder what type of decisions I would make at school when my brain is still developing and I'm constantly in survival mode?*
- *How would I feel in school if my perspective was never included?* (My Reality)

- *Why wouldn't we explore multiple perspectives and learning styles while learning?*

When you begin to place yourself in the mindset of your scholars, you can better understand some of the decisions they make or behaviors that are displayed. It doesn't mean you will agree with your scholars on everything, but everyone is on a journey to find their true selves. Adopting this mentality allows educators to take on the perspective of seeing their scholars as human beings who are *qualified to make mistakes*.

In my classroom, our team was able to point to the failures and challenging moments that we experienced in life as opportunities to grow. We normalized and welcomed setbacks as opportunities to learn and grow from, but it took lots of intentional conversations and activities. The mindset part of this is often overlooked because through setbacks you will see some things that don't make you a proud teacher. You must reset and readjust often to deal with the millions of decisions an educator must make. When you create that safe, nonjudgmental environment, scholars can release some of the pressure that operating in a highly structured school setting brings. Now scholars can put their guard down immediately, knowing there isn't a need for a false sense of perfection.

Once you establish this environment, you instantly build a level of trust which becomes the foundation of your classroom management. Of course, no educational setting is perfect, but that's the beauty of being an educator; you really are shaping the minds and spaces of young people. Neither scholars nor teachers will be perfect, but setting your foundation allows for everyone to grow with one another. You must start immediately by being fair, firm, and consistent. Show your scholars that as adults we can also make mistakes in the classroom and through vulnerability learn to overcome those mistakes together. You also need to show them that you have high expectations of them and for yourself. By establishing this, you have created a scholar-centered classroom. You have eliminated a tone of teacher-self ego, which is the declaration that only I-AM in control. Instead, focus on creating a culture of *we* are in this *together*. Setting this tone will allow scholars to buy in because you have allowed vulnerability to co-exist and not be a one-hit wonder.

Dr. Erica Glover, author of Centering Student Voice: A Guide for Cultivating Emotionally Intelligent Educators and Culturally Responsive Classrooms, analyzes the topic of creating scholar-centered classrooms very well. You don't have to prove your authenticity and accountability to your scholars; your actions do (Glover, 2022). Classrooms with great relationships are not classrooms that just allow scholars to do whatever they want. They are spaces that encourage scholars and teachers to be who they are while learning and growing together as humans.

Scholars often perceive school as a place where every adult is perfect and feel like kids can't make mistakes.

FLY ABOVE FAILURE

Flying above failure is a mantra that was used by myself, the scholars, and the teaching assistants in the classroom because mistakes need to be encouraged. This is another part of classroom culture that should not be a one-time thing because it will take repetition and time to develop this mindset collectively. Earlier I mentioned the vulnerability of identifying and sharing my failures as an educator and as a regular person. What about how failure looks in the homes of your scholars and in their communities? How is failure addressed in other classrooms in your school? Please remember that there are many sources of influence on the mindsets of scholars beyond your classroom. This is your chance to locate change agents that exist in the school or in the community that can be resources for you and your scholars. Collaborating with veteran teachers or community veterans that are very active can provide a level of support that teachers really need. Family environment and support play a crucial role in shaping a scholar's mindset. Supportive parents or guardians who encourage learning and provide a stable home environment can greatly contribute to a positive academic mindset. *Supportive parents or guardians will look and feel different for every family* so it is important for you not to paint everyone with the same brush when it comes to your idea of what it should look like. School environment and relationships also have an impact on scholar's mindset and educational approach. A positive, inclusive, and safe environment can inspire scholars and positively influence their attitudes toward self-improvement. Peer influence and social interactions are arguably a heavy determinant in a scholar's mindset especially during adolescence. Positive peer influence can boost confidence, motivation, and interest in extracurricular activities. Conversely, negative peer pressure can lead to a detrimental mindset and disinterest in school all together. Positive or negative experiences are all part of the developmental process and both can be very beneficial to individual development.

I have experienced many hidden benefits of teaching during my time in a "Self-Contained" unit. Our teaching approach was acknowledging that we had a built-in community of support with all the adults communicating the same messages. This is one practice that allowed our classroom space to establish solidarity with our scholars.

Scholars need to fail. I'm going to say that again scholars need to fail. Often attributed to Dr. A.P.J. Abdul Kalam stated that the acronym for

F.A.I.L., stands for "first attempt in learning". How can a person build resilience if they never learn to deal with adversity? The disciplinary policies in schools are major contributors to the school-to-prison pipeline because most of the time they aren't solution-based. How a scholar responds to experiencing failure and how failure is approached by their educators impacts how their mind is shaped. Helping scholars redefine their definition of failure will help eliminate a need for only punitive consequences that are often administered when a scholar has displayed a negative response to the embarrassing feeling of getting a question wrong in front of their peers. Scholars pay attention to you as their leader and watch your actions more than they listen to your words. If you reinforce that you're here to support scholars who identify their mistakes and failures then hold them accountable with love (*tough love*), you embed this mindset into your teaching practice and allow space for everyone to hold each other accountable. You may be thinking "How is the teacher supposed to do all of this stuff and teach the content?" When you make lifelong learning a top priority along with your content, the two will become interchangeable.

Teachers often, and not purposely, have a mindset of I'm the smartest and I'm in charge, but this is not a growth mindset. It would be wise for teachers to consider the power of utilizing all the voices and perspectives within a shared space to create a thriving, healthy educational space. There is power in empowering others! Flying above failure takes those moments of learning with our scholars and makes the impact of those moments more authentic. Of course, as the adult in the room, you are an expert. You likely have more life experiences in which you have learned and grown from, but scholars are masters of their own experiences, too. Many times, they have experienced things that teachers can only surmise. When teachers allow scholars to bring their experiences into the classroom, to talk about them, and then allow those experiences to teach everyone, the learning environment becomes relatable for everyone.

Thinking back to your learning experience, do you recall being a perfect scholar who never made mistakes, never got in trouble, sat there with your hands neatly folded, were always paying attention, and engaged in every lesson? If so, then maybe you are in the wrong profession. This is because education is a place where people should be comfortable with the process of learning new information and learning about themselves.

I'm not saying that extremely engaged scholars don't exist. I'm also not saying that your scholars won't push you past your limits. The reality is, that everyone makes mistakes and young people will try to take advantage of adults. Instead of approaching this as a bad thing, view it as an opportunity. You've gone to school, earned credentials, and put in lots of work, but the speed of global evolution technologically, digitally, environmentally, economically, culturally, and socially has only increased. It's time that the educational profession adjusts with the times.

Every adult was once young and learned to work through issues to make it to where they currently are. In life, constant learning needs to take place, and it usually comes from perceived failures. Use failure as a tool in your classroom and be on the lookout for success stories that your scholars will come back and share with you.

FLY ABOVE FAILURE SUCCESS STORIES

- **Muhammad Ali**, originally named Cassius Clay, faced racial prejudice and controversy for his outspoken views, particularly against the Vietnam War. Ali was willing to sacrifice his boxing career to take a stand for what he believed in. He went on to become one of the most celebrated boxers and humanitarians of all time.

- **Katherine Johnson, Dorothy Vaughan, and Mary Jackson**, also known as the "Hidden Figures," were highlighted in a film that showcased their extraordinary talents and contributions to space exploration. They used resilience and determination to overcome societal barriers of heavy racism and sexism, constantly proving their capabilities and worth in environments where they were often underestimated.
- **Thomas Edison went** through many trials and tribulations to have a role in the invention of the light bulb. Through resilience, he went on to hold over 1,000 patents, including the invention of the phonograph and the modern light bulb.
- **Ermias Joseph Asghedom**, known professionally as "Nipsey Hussle," grew up in and around gang activity. At 14 years old, he left home and experienced multiple levels of adversity that inspired him to use music as a channel for expression. Nipsey went on to release the record "Victory Lap," which was nominated for a Grammy Award and has influenced many entrepreneurs to embrace the challenge of overcoming adversity.

Your willingness as an educational professional to use failure as a tool to reinforce the power of resilience can be the catalyst that propels one of your scholars into a global change agent, similar to those mentioned above.

THE ABILITY TO LOOK IN THE MIRROR.

An educational professional who practices critical reflection can properly identify potential growth areas within themselves and their scholars. Critical reflection in educational settings is often used to enhance learning and development, encouraging scholars to think deeply about their learning experiences. Three areas of critical reflection that can have a large impact on individual growth are **becoming lifelong learners, critically thinking for themselves**, and **self awareness** (Glover, 2022).

Becoming a lifelong learner challenges you to reflect on one's own beliefs, assumptions, and biases to see how they impact thoughts and actions. Imagine talking about this process with your scholars in a way that helps them relate to perceived failure as part of the process.

Critically thinking for self is when an individual can integrate new knowledge so that future actions and decisions can be combined with existing knowledge.

Self-Awareness is one area that educational professionals look for when assessing a scholar's growth but is also part of the quest of the adults, there is no specific age that an individual learns to put all of their experiences together. One of my growth areas as a teacher was my approach to providing positive scholar feedback on assignments. I was the king of building up all scholars' personal swag. As teachers, it is our desire and responsibility to provide meaningful feedback to help scholars grow. But early in my career, teaching Language Arts, my scholars shared with me that the way that I was communicating with them was destroying their confidence. High school Language Arts requires extensive writing assignments. Contrary to the beliefs of many, scholars labeled "Emotionally Disabled, Learning Disabled, Low" and all the other stereotypical names are capable of writing essays and many other requested tasks. One key is knowing that all your scholars start at different levels and can potentially produce different versions of a final product to display mastery.

Here was a common mistake that I learned from. Earlier in my career, when my scholars turned in their essays, I failed to immediately identify the positive elements or acknowledge the fact that they had even completed the assignment. Instead, I would instantly begin correcting their mistakes, which seemed to be the correct thing to do at the time. Since my scholars felt comfortable talking about areas of growth during our daily morning family meetings, they shared how they interpreted my feedback. Many of them felt that I would immediately tear down their essays without providing constructive criticism. Without presenting the feedback using the *sandwich approach*, which involves opening your feedback with positive comments, then an area of growth opportunity, and finally ending with positive comments. By choosing not to use the sandwich approach I potentially could have worsened the mentality of my scholars. This seemed to really bother them especially given the way their school experience has turned out so far. Collectively we discussed a possible solution that we could work on together. You won't have to bend and adjust every time one of your scholars suggests but using critical reflection to guide your decision making is an important step in how you determine the approach that best fits the situation.

Upon receiving the feedback from my scholars, I could have been conceited failing to receive this valuable feedback, but I recognized it as an obvious growth opportunity for me. I had already established from day one that mistakes were going to be made by everyone (including myself) and we would have to hold each other accountable by speaking on it. What do you think happened to my scholars on the inside when I told them that they were right and that I needed to get better at one of my struggling areas? By the scholars calling me out and having collective dialogue about it, they felt more comfortable with me, and it positively affected their confidence in writing. At the beginning of the year, many of the scholars weren't very strong writers, according to educational standards. As a result, their low scores greatly impacted their confidence. By building their confidence in writing early in the school year, I knew I would be able to push them more and more as the school year progressed. It's possible for an educator to defeat a student's mindset, Dr. Bettina Love calls it *spirit murdering*, causing students to never feel like they are capable of recognizing their genius (Love, 2019). This is a battle that we have control over.

I knew that I had to be vulnerable for the sake of my own personal growth and for my scholars' growth. A teacher that embraces their role as a facilitator takes on the mindset of searching for growth opportunities because it creates an inclusive environment. I believe that all scholars want to be academically successful and have varying definitions of what success even looks like. Allow them to share their version with you. In turn, they will likely become receptive to your assistance with reshaping their success definition, especially if you let them help you grow as well. My scholars considered their completed essays as a success for themselves because they wouldn't have even made the attempt to start them in the past. The experience of receiving my scholars' feedback on my own feedback process confirmed that we were all learning and growing together. I was learning that failure was just like the acronym said, it was a *First Attempt In Learning*. Now, ask yourself, how many times do your scholars make suggestions regarding your teaching style? Do you listen to them? Education doesn't demand that you implement everything your scholars suggest but the fact that they feel comfortable enough to address their concerns with you speaks to the type of environment you've created.

BENEFITS OF REFLECTION

Some key takeaways that scholars can take from learning the importance of reflection include exhibiting authenticity (*Just be who you are*), displaying courage, and accepting imperfections in yourself and others. Scholars will usually buy what the teacher is selling if they present it with genuine love. Remember, scholars are expecting their teacher to be an educational expert. I challenge you to show them an example of executing theory to practice.

Demonstrating your expertise in the lifelong learning process can surprise your scholars who think that teachers don't have flaws like all human beings. This was a game-changer for my scholars' Social-Emotional growth, and it was a very important part of showcasing mistakes as acceptable and welcomed in our classroom. It's critical to the trust-building process that educators can admit their mistakes so that the classroom becomes a welcoming space. Always remember that scholars are experts of their own experiences.

SKITS ARE LIT! REVERSE THE ROLES AND LEARN TOGETHER.

One of the most successful techniques we used to highlight failure in a fun and engaging way was participating in skits. Skits are a highly effective practice for teachers to help scholars fly above failure in the classroom.

Teachers can use skits to encourage scholars to demonstrate how they've grasped a new concept. The formula we used for our skits resonated with the culture of our classroom: teachers and scholars swapped roles and were tasked with portraying each other. Teachers role-played as their scholars, while scholars took turns leading the classroom, scholars love being the teacher or facilitator. Scholars focused not on teaching content but specifically on illustrating their perceptions of your tone, mannerisms, and approach toward them daily.

This activity can transform outlooks on failure for several reasons:

- Scholars feel more connected when they can candidly point out areas for improvement, fostering vulnerability and connection.
- They often emphasize your most noticeable growth opportunities, serving as a reflective tool.
- You get the chance to humorously exaggerate scholar behaviors (strongly recommended for teacher revenge).
- Everyone enjoys some of the best laughs of the year.

I recommend doing this activity once every quarter; it never gets old on either end. Initially intended for perspective-taking, we discovered it had deeper implications. This activity injects humor into perceived failure, allowing scholars to lower their guard and demonstrating your nonchalance toward perceived failure. Whether positive or negative, they'll make sure to emphasize their conclusions about your teaching style and personality. You'll learn where you're still learning in the eyes of your scholars.

During the skits, be loud, be distracting, but above all, embody your scholars' personalities. Become the scholar who always blurts out thoughts and interrupts—you're embodying them while they attempt to be you. Let them experience the impact of their behavior and choices from your perspective.

This fun activity isn't meant to be negative or put anyone down; it's about understanding each other. It's likely to strengthen your relationships by creating discussion points for improvement and emphasizing choices and behaviors everyone can acknowledge and work to change. After these role-play sessions, review the positive and negative examples of perceived failure and collectively discuss them. This allows the class to create a success plan to overcome failure together.

Before implementing skits, transparency is key: you must have already established an inclusive environment. This isn't an activity you can spring on your scholars and expect success. We had conversations beforehand about focusing on mannerisms and tone during specific situations. We ensured scholars didn't take responses personally, knowing how some react when called out. We successfully conducted this activity in a self-contained classroom with scholars deemed most behaviorally challenging. I emphasize this point to illustrate that, regardless of potential baggage, diligent groundwork matters. We never had to stop this activity due to a negative response; I believe this was because every adult was genuine about our own shortcomings and willing to bring them to light.

Here are 3 ground rules that will help you if you decide to implement this activity:

1. Communicate with your class on the first day of meeting them that you aren't perfect and the entire year everyone will grow together.

2. Communicate with your class that you are planning to grow through things together and that growth will come from pointing out the areas of growth for everyone.

3. Use professional judgment and read the room. If you have the activity planned and it doesn't appear like your scholars are in the right frame of mind, then wait until that moment presents itself.

Both Scholars and adults can have struggles with emotional intelligence. We expect teachers and scholars to be tasteful when attempting this activity. We wouldn't want anyone to feel threatened or uncomfortable, but this is something that is established and controlled by the environment the teacher creates.

There's a saying that goes *"The greatness of humanity is not in being human, but in being humane"* by Mahatma Gandhi. That quote holds a lot of weight because we must consider the fact that we are all learning and growing on our own continuum. We need to be realistic in our self-reflection. Control what you can control is some of the greatest advice any teacher can implement.

REFLECTION QUESTIONS

- Are scholars afraid to fail in my class?
- How would my scholars describe the energy toward failure in my classroom?
- Do I share personal strengths and areas of growth with scholars daily? *How can I age-appropriately provide details about my positive and negative real-life events?*
- *What type of vulnerable stories have I shared with my scholars that have helped them connect to me beyond a surface level?*
- *What types of things should I share with my scholars but am choosing to hold back?*
- Do I believe my scholars view me as a teacher that never messes up?
- *Do I consistently acknowledge my mistakes in front of my scholars?*

I HATE SCIENCE!
I LOVE YOUR CLASS THOUGH.

LIFE IN THE TRENCHES

Before diving into Chapter 2, I want to share another story from my teaching experience. Being a self-contained intervention specialist meant teaching all core subjects (Math, Science, Social Studies, History), and a Social Emotional Learning (SEL) elective within the unit. For other electives (gym, art, music, etc.), our scholars earned credits by attending classes outside with the general education population. It mirrored the school-to-prison pipeline due to the setup and issues with standardized testing, graduation rates, and attendance, which led Ohio to mandate transformation.

During this overhaul, we adopted a co-teaching model to improve the school's climate and culture. Co-teaching involved two educational experts in the room, sometimes with paraprofessionals, depending on the need. The Individualized Education Program (IEP) determined where scholars received educational services. I partnered with Rebecca Butler, an exceptional Science educator. Mrs. Butler, a white woman, exemplified fairness, firmness, and consistency in her classroom approach. Before co-teaching, she frequently visited the self-contained classroom, appreciating our projects and rapport with scholars.

One year, due to a surge in freshmen enrollment for the self-contained class, I had the choice to teach them myself or collaborate with Rebecca. Given my comfort in English and need for growth in Science, teaming up with Rebecca was an obvious choice. We discussed her desire to deepen connections with scholars amidst the literacy-focused teaching directive. We decided to integrate journaling into our curriculum. Scholars wrote in their journals three times weekly, with flexible topics; sometimes specific, sometimes chosen by scholars. They were also encouraged to include personal well-being updates or urgent needs on sticky notes, allowing us to provide additional support.

This initiative unexpectedly revealed scholars' personal challenges and positive experiences, often overlooked. Scholars embraced journaling, and feedback was overwhelmingly positive. We engaged in discussions to ensure scholars understood the purpose and routine of journaling.

scholars from various classes praised the positive impact of having an outlet for their feelings. Despite not always enjoying Physical Science lessons, especially those without hands-on labs, they valued our concern for their well-being over subject matter. Contextualizing our population, 98% of the school qualified for free lunch, with average incomes in the zip code significantly lower than suburban areas, compounded by real issues like violent crime. However, their living conditions didn't dictate a deficit approach to their education.

SECRET 2:
MAKE KIDS ACTUALLY LIKE COMING TO YOUR ROOM

"I've learned that people will forget what you said, people will forget what you did, but people will never forget how you made them feel."
Maya Angelou

A CLASSROOM COMMUNITY

The second secret in *"7 Secrets for Beating Educator Burnout"* is creating an environment that kids actually want to be part of. This can happen by simply creating a space the kids like coming to. Yes, I know that it sounds simple, but the reality is oftentimes scholars do not want to go to class, for a plethora of reasons. A lot of them are self-inflicted by the scholars' conscience, some of them are environmentally inflicted, and some of them are teacher inflicted. Of course, you can add in social media, peer influence, and more. The reality is you never know what influences the mind of your scholars unless you ask. One thing that you can control is what happens in your classroom! Kids can hate the content that you have to teach but enjoy being in your presence if you are cultivating the right environment. To ensure that scholars feel welcome and valued inside *of* your classroom, it is important to build a classroom community and amplify scholar voices. This type of classroom has accountability, tough love, and compassion.

During my first year as a licensed Behavioral Intervention Specialist, I was assigned to the Severe Behavioral Intervention School that housed the most intensive behavioral scholars grades K-8 in Akron, Ohio. This was a building that many people were afraid to enter. The stories about it and its reputation were interesting to me, mostly because I was already subbing there consistently prior to being licensed and my perspective and experiences differed from most educators. To be fair, the building appearance presented itself as intimidating and a majority of scholar behaviors were extremely severe. The school was built in 1926, so by the time I was teaching there (2010), it was 84 years old. It hadn't been well maintained and didn't have air conditioning. Only some of the heaters worked, the lights were dim, and it didn't have the most welcoming atmosphere, to say the least. As a teacher, I was charged with coming to this building and creating magic with scholars that barely even made it to the building on most days. Scholars were cursing at each other and teachers, fights were breaking out at any given time, and there were even time-out rooms that looked like small jail cells. There is no need to sugarcoat the details of the environment; however, that doesn't mean learning couldn't take place in a classroom environment that was scholar centered. It's all about the mindset.

Let me tell you about how my year teaching at a severe Behavioral Intervention School began. During the first 5 minutes as a first-year teacher, I went to the cafeteria/gym to pick up my scholars so we could start the year off. They were eating while some of the other teachers completed their last-minute prep. I remember thinking the first-day-of-school conditions were crazy. It was probably 110 degrees in the building because it was late August and there was no air conditioning except for in 2 offices and the timeout rooms. The scholars had been eating breakfast for about 20 minutes and although they were being fed, the intense temperature was a major setup for destruction. We made it about halfway to our classroom when, **BOOM**, a fight broke out between who I later found out were my scholars with the two strongest personalities. They wasted no time in letting everyone know who the alpha male in the class was. Being that I had previously subbed in the building and was aware of many of the scholars' manipulation tactics and hustles, I knew what to expect. I had a hunch that one of the scholars had intentionally started the fight so he could start his day in a timeout room with air conditioning. He had a full stomach and was probably ready to go back to sleep like he was still on summer vacation. Behaviors are true communicators and don't always show up in the pleasant ways that we desire. I could have been mentally shaken up over what happened. I could have been frustrated and transferred all my frustration to the rest of the scholars, but I didn't. I chose to control what I could at the time and moved forward with what I had. I knew that I was going to have access to the two young men later at which point I would address them properly. The most powerful thing I did was allow the other scholars to experience starting the school year with the *best teacher in the world.*

I entered the building focused on developing relationships with my scholars because I wanted to treat them like people, not scholars with extreme behaviors. I understood that before any learning could take place, the scholars needed to know who I was, and I needed to know who they were. Their school records and Individualized Education Plans (IEP) had plenty of details about their behavioral struggles, but I knew that I needed more information to help me gain the control and influence I would need to be impactful.

Once the scholars were settled in the classroom, we opened with conversations and games that I could use as teachable moments. Playing games during class can give educators an opportunity to weave in curriculum. You can use content strategies to provide feedback and allow your scholars to start putting down their guard. The games brought on various emotions that I knew my scholars struggled to manage, but it allowed me to address the event that occurred during the first five minutes after my introduction to them in a professional manner. I didn't punish them or administer consequences to the entire class so that I could *set the tone*. My psychological approach was to allow them to play games, have fun, and learn by doing. I knew that if any of the scholars in the room needed extra redirection, it would have been given. During the game play, some scholars became frustrated, angry, and jealous of their peers. I used their reactions during the games to point out some focus areas of *our* classroom. This tactic always worked when I taught middle schoolers. Trust takes longer than a day for human beings to develop and goes deeper than titles, so remember that you'll have to pull your sleeves up and dig in during those early days, weeks, and months of the school year. You never know what situation or environment the scholars may have recently experienced. Be mindful not to approach relationship building from a deficit mindset. Learn to take the circumstances for what they are and adjust your expectations and actions accordingly. Creating a classroom community is a yearlong commitment so try not to think of this vital step as *"a first week of school activity"* or another item on your lesson plan. Scholars need you to love them all the time even through discipline and accountability. When you learn how to love scholars and hold them accountable you have created something special.

SCHOLAR-LED CLASSROOM IDENTITY

During that same school year, we agreed as a team to create a positive identity within our classrooms. I was working with 6th, 7th, and 8th-grade scholars who were all in the same classroom. For this specific school year, every classroom was required to come up with their own classroom name. Instead of approaching this practice from a deficit mindset and wondering if my scholars would want to participate, I immediately thought about ways to involve them in the process. I knew from previous interactions that the scholars in my building felt voiceless and marginalized by educators. My goal was to help them gain individual and collective voices. The name that my scholars and I eventually chose was **Team HOOD!**

We decided to transform the term "hood," which by societal standards negatively references inner-city neighborhoods like ours. Having been raised in similar neighborhoods to those of my scholars, I understood how stereotypes could shape people's views of urban areas. We sat down and had a lengthy conversation about "The Hood". This discussion helped us assign new meaning to the name. They learned the meaning of an acronym, and together we created a "hood" acronym. I didn't explicitly tell the scholars that our conversation was also academic in nature, but they were working as a team, problem-solving, and thinking critically about their neighborhood—things that many believed couldn't be done at our school.

To be transparent, during this discussion, there were disagreements among the scholars, and they weren't always discussed in a professional manner. At times, things got serious, and phrases like **"fuck what you talking about," "you don't know shit for real,"** and **"naw that shit don't work on my side of town"** were said. But despite this, the foundation for growth opportunities was established. Now was my time to work my educational magic.

My task was to foster growth from where they were. I wasn't going to allow scholars to curse in my class all day, every day, but I also couldn't let that bother me from the outset. I knew what I was dealing with and had detailed plans on how to instill the norms and values I wanted. Addressing foul language prematurely would have set me up for failure in establishing connections with scholars. I could have lectured them on why it wasn't appropriate, but many of my scholars faced real-life situations where that was *normal dialogue.* Instead, I connected their experience of constant profanity to potential insights into actions of people in the community, particularly their families.

I used what I learned through Carmelo Anthony and a foundation he founded called **"Holding Our Own Destiny" or HOOD**. My scholars could relate to a multi-millionaire basketball player from the "hood" of Baltimore, so I used his experience to validate my perspective. This allowed us to change the negative way we viewed the hood. We began discussing all the positive aspects occurring within "our" community that weren't widely known or talked about. This naturally led us into the conversation about profanity. We also talked about the power of personal decision-making and the essential requirements needed to transition from the "bad school".

This conversation provided a timely and valuable opportunity for me to build connections with some of the scholars, as a resident of the city's West side—many of them lived on other sides. Let's be honest, most of the teachers working in the inner-city commute from the suburbs; 80% of them are white women. This gives teachers an automatic opportunity to view that as an asset or a liability. As an educator, sharing about the neighborhood you live in or grew up in provides a guaranteed opportunity to learn from and with your scholars. This can promote bonding over commonalities or learning from differences. Scholars love hearing about the different life perspectives their teachers bring, as long as theirs aren't demeaned in the process. In this instance, there is no need for correct spelling, grammar, reading comprehension, or memorization of math formulas. There is a lot to be gained from good old-fashioned conversation where the kids are actually teaching you.

BRING THE HOOD TO YOUR CLASSROOM (INVEST TIME IN THE COMMUNITY)

The reality of marginalized communities is that many local people are battling systemic inequity issues such as stable housing, food deserts, racism as a public health crisis, and more. Activists from these neighborhoods are actively striving for change and are deeply engaged in community efforts. When you choose to teach in such an environment, you're in a unique position to bring the community or the "hood" into your classroom. This practice offers a genuine opportunity to invest time in the community you serve. It requires multiple efforts to connect with community leaders and enhance the long-term positive impact of your teaching experience.

Engaging with youth service organizations enables you to become part of the village. By establishing these connections, you can involve your family in community activities like shopping and attending local events, establishing a visible presence in the community where you teach. As a result, you'll encounter scholars and their families outside of school, gradually diminishing any biases, known or unknown. You'll forge connections with real people beyond the classroom setting and cultivate allies and collaborators to rely on. I understand educators have personal lives outside of work hours, but even small changes like these can profoundly impact your classroom in ways you might not expect.

Teachers gain a significant advantage in connecting with scholars when they are seen beyond their role as educators. Actively participating in the community can add that extra layer of connection. Educators should actively counteract any negative stereotypes scholars may hold, such as the belief that teachers are solely focused on delivering curriculum and meeting assessment goals, rather than caring about scholars as individuals. One effective strategy to combat these stereotypes is by integrating elements of the hood into your classroom.

Establishing connections between scholars' personal environments and the learning environment fosters reciprocal relationships that stimulate curiosity. For instance, if scholars know that during History class they will discuss and write about events in their neighborhood, influential figures impacting their community, and connect these to current events, they are more likely to attend and engage. By focusing on the school community, you highlight topics and events directly relevant to scholars, helping them navigate school-related anxieties.

There may be occasions when addressing your scholars' mental health or offering words of encouragement becomes necessary. In times of community tragedy, when the school lacks sufficient counselors to meet scholars needs, community leaders may step in to bridge the gap. Sometimes, scholars may prefer discussing issues with community leaders rather than counselors who lack ties to the scholars or their community. On several occasions, scholars have told me, "Mr. Smith, I don't trust any other teachers in the building because they never talk about our neighborhood. I trust your classroom!" This trust in the inclusive learning environment we collectively created didn't mean I had all the answers, but it was a tangible outcome of my willingness to listen to my scholars' concerns without judgment.

Therefore, if you decide to implement practices like naming your classroom, consider allowing scholars to contribute to or even lead this process. When scholars are involved, they take pride in and feel ownership of both the process and the outcome. Once completed, your project will have transformed your classroom into a space every scholar will want to visit and feel a part of. As the leader, it's crucial to learn to delegate some control and authority; empowering young minds ultimately enhances your own influence.

Food For Thought: The naming of your classroom activity was used for middle school scholars.

THE 3 C'S CURRICULUM, CULTURE, AND COMMUNITY!

The current system of education has had very minimal changes that would align with the needs of 21st century learners. Kids do not care if you are an expert in the curriculum if you can't relate it to them and make it meaningful. We are aware of ways to discover some of the things that scholars know. But, what is your procedure for finding out what scholars don't know but are curious about learning? When you start to find out this information, you can use it as leverage to help you work less on managing behaviors and more on establishing a culture of wellness check-ins when scholars first arrive in your classroom. Although you have deadlines to meet and your plate is overflowing, establishing a classroom culture can help eliminate small fires and steer the climate of your classroom.

Once you cultivate a classroom culture, a visitor can pop in and feel the presence of the three C's and determine the pulse of your classroom environment quickly. A sense of community is critical when young people are trying to navigate life's obstacles. Think about the curriculum that you are charged to teach and think about your scholars. If you use the curriculum provided to you, will all your scholars feel represented in that curriculum? Let's be honest, the answer is no for most scholars who don't identify as white males. Many textbooks show a lack of multicultural information which provides an opportunity for teachers to bring in multiple perspectives. Representation is very powerful. If you want to ensure engagement, then you must find ways to make representation part of your curriculum planning priorities. This helps scholars feel like they are part of the class. I'm not saying you don't use your professional expertise but if I really want scholars to practice a specific writing task it would be beneficial for me to use an interesting hook. The adult learning theory of Malcolm Knowles says when an adult doesn't feel like they are a part of something, they are not going to want to participate, so why do we think it is different for the kids? If scholars are not participating in class, they are most likely not turning in assignments. If they aren't turning in assignments, then that also means that they're not making good marks. This is the meaning of authentic student relationships being the key to academic success, which takes work. Part of the work that is in your control includes analyzing your curriculum standards, having conversations with colleagues and mentors, and doing extra planning on the front end. Although this is likely a part of your current requirements from your school, embedding these action steps early in the year could influence your entire teaching experience for the rest of the year and give you *more time* on the back end.

BLENDING THE C'S
PRACTICAL EXAMPLE:

One project that stands out during my time in the classroom was one that I created for high school scholars on argumentative essays. We used

Project Based Learning to combine English and Social Studies. We used the bias and credibility standards from Social Studies to write argumentative essays on why our current textbooks were not a credible source of information on the duration of lynchings. The textbook only provided one small paragraph on lynchings and the scholars challenged the way the information was presented. Scholars were excited to learn about African American culture outside of Black History Month. This project allowed us to create a community of support inside our classroom environment. This project connected to the 3 C's because of the following:

- The textbook curriculum was very general and one-sided, so we decided to explore it deeper.
- We learned more about African American culture using the internet and information from scholarly journals that traditional textbooks often exclude.
- We established a community of learning with one another by acknowledging that none of us were experts in this field.
- Eliminating non-credible and opinion-based information to put in our argument was a very fun part of the process.
- scholars were engaged and encouraged with lots of learning taking place, we eliminated distractions as best as we could (they still were Emotionally Disabled teenagers).
- The 3 Cs allowed for everyone to learn together. There weren't any extreme behavioral incidents during this specific project.

Completing this project proved that when the curriculum doesn't take advantage of having multiple voices and perspectives there is a huge opportunity for the 3 C's to be integrated into your teaching experience. This will require you to put your guard down and become a facilitator, have fun admitting you're not the expert and enjoy strengthening student-teacher trust building. Seeking out these opportunities will be game-changing pivots to your teaching practice.

BIAS STANDARDS

1. ***Identification of Bias:*** *scholars are taught to identify different types of bias in sources, including political, cultural, economic, and social biases. They learn to recognize the influence of the author's perspective on the information presented.*

2. ***Analysis of Perspective:*** *scholars analyze how different perspectives influence the interpretation of events and issues. This includes understanding the historical context and the background of the source.*

3. ***Comparison of Multiple Sources:*** *scholars compare multiple sources on the same topic to identify differing viewpoints and biases. This helps them understand how bias can shape the portrayal of events and issues.*

4. ***Evaluation of Arguments:*** *scholars evaluate the strength and validity of arguments presented in sources, taking into account the presence of bias and the use of evidence.*

CREDIBILITY STANDARDS

1. ***Source Evaluation:*** *scholars are taught to evaluate the credibility of sources by considering the author's qualifications, the publication's reputation, and the date of the information. They learn to distinguish between primary and secondary sources and understand the value and limitations of each.*

2. ***Evidence-Based Analysis:*** *scholars analyze the evidence provided in sources, assessing its relevance, accuracy, and sufficiency. They learn to identify credible sources that provide well-supported, factual information.*

3. ***Corroboration of Information:*** *scholars corroborate information by cross-referencing multiple credible sources. This practice helps them verify the accuracy of the information and recognize discrepancies.*

4. ***Understanding Propaganda and Misinformation:*** *scholars learn to identify propaganda, misinformation, and disinformation. They develop skills to critically evaluate information found in various media, including digital and social media.*

COMMUNITY RESOURCES

As you navigate the task of connecting to the community, you are serving an important question for teachers to ask themselves. "What community resources are available to my scholars *and* I?" It's extremely beneficial for teachers to explore community resources such as small businesses, community members, and public-serving institutions. Connecting with these resources and including them in your mission to create and bring forth change can have a sizable impact on your planning process. Business owners and community stakeholders love to collaborate with the schools in their communities but don't always know how to get involved. So, consider finding ways to gain access to these assets.

For this powerful reason, I advocate for *Project-Based Learning*. According to *Boston University Center for Teaching and Learning,* "*Project Based Learning*" (*PBL*) involves scholars designing, developing, and constructing hands-on solutions to a problem. The educational value of *PBL* is that it aims to build scholars' creative capacity to work through difficult or ill-structured problems, commonly in small teams." This learning style promotes inquisitive learning through scholar voice and allows teachers to make meaningful connections to the curriculum. The value of connecting with specific people and community organizations increases when you can bring them into your classroom and gain necessary support. It changes the way scholars view you, from just a teacher who's visiting from a different community to a community advocate. As you prioritize discussing things that your scholars see taking place on a day-to-day basis, it allows them to create meaningful solutions for themselves and others. This lets scholars know that you genuinely care about the community that you teach in and you're making it a point to be part of the change. This can help build mutual respect and trust inside and out of the classroom. My goal isn't to tell educators to spend most of their after-school hours in the community in which they likely don't reside. The goal is to help them understand that going into the community continuously and collaborating with others will be beneficial to your classroom environment which simultaneously helps everyone.

When it comes to finalizing your lessons, each curriculum unit has themes. Work with colleagues to discuss how to connect your lesson's big ideas to alternative areas. The lesson's theme provides an opportunity to make worldly connections. How do the lesson themes connect to situations that are currently taking place in the world? What are the similarities and differences? How do we create change so that we don't continue to see negative cycles? Teachers have the opportunity to impress young minds. Take advantage of that opportunity by making continuous real-world connections. Allow scholars to voice their opinions on how they see these problems and suggest possible solutions for these problems.

This will allow your classroom to flow and for you to become the facilitator your scholars are looking for. These are all valuable secrets when it comes creating the classroom that your kids will want to come to.

REFLECTION QUESTIONS:

- Do I allow scholar voice to accompany decision-making in my classroom?
- Do I attend community events outside of school hours, besides sports?
- Do I bring community issues into my classroom?
- Do I Connect The Curriculum, Culture, and Community to my scholars?
- Do I provide an opportunity for my scholars to check-in and acknowledge their feelings daily?
- Do I constantly use examples of everyday life scenarios to help scholars make connections to classroom content?

PHONES ARE A DISTRACTION.

TEACHING IN THE TRENCHES

Including student voice when it comes to setting up your classroom management needs to be a non-negotiable tool. Teachers should give students an opportunity to provide input on classroom operations. During our return to in-person learning post-Covid, one of my classes really struggled with the cell phone policy. My students knew that I didn't play when it came to phones, and they also knew I didn't like repeating myself. They were aware that I had very high expectations of them, especially if they were choosing not to pay attention and allow themselves to be distracted. Honestly, I never had cell phone issues in my class because I made it a point to keep students engaged by including them in parts of my teaching plan. I had all the standard tools like classroom rules and expectations and a chart of how it connected to Positive Behavior Intervention and Support (PBIS). I did all that was asked of me because I saw the benefit of having structure in the classroom. I also knew from experience that when something isn't working, you must pivot, regardless of how much you thought the original plan was going to work.

Let me let you in on a secret: every scholar that I had this particular year was selected for my class due to experiencing major struggles the previous year. I had requested all of them to be in my class (You can tell I love this challenge). They were a targeted group of what the world of education would refer to as "At Risk" students. Extensive experience in teaching students with Emotional Disabilities helped me to dismiss the majority of my stereotypical views. Every class presents its unique set of challenges, and these students were no different. One class specifically experienced continuous cell phone distraction and we had to have a "family meeting". Family meetings were a common practice that I used to address an issue collectively. I adopted this practice in my early years of teaching in severe behavioral self-contained units because it was part of our daily routine. It was my belief that if no learning is taking place, then a conversation needs to be held with everyone involved.

During this family meeting I reminded my students that we had rules and expectations for the classroom that everyone previously agreed on. One of the rules was no cell phones unless granted permission by the teacher. I was set in my mind that I wasn't giving warnings for cell phones because it was something we often discussed, and they knew how it negatively impacted student engagement. I asked my students what they thought we should do when I must stop their instruction and address the cell phones. The scholars suggested that they get a warning first, even though the classroom norms didn't include this practice. We already established what the cell phone policy was so why would I consider something else? I really didn't want to at all BUT teachers have to pick their battles AND find ways to collaborate with their students. WE talked and came to the agreement that students would get a warning if I saw their cell phone. It was imperative that I drop my ego on this one. The second time I witnessed a student being distracted by their phone the student would have to put it into the cell phone box on my desk. I jokingly told them that I didn't want their raggedy phones with cracked screens and I had the best phone in the room anyway. We all agreed on this amendment to our agreement and the end result was if a student tried to fight me on the rule of putting their phone into the box, their peers would instantly hold them accountable. The most famous saying became "Just put your phone in the box, Mr. Smith doesn't want your raggedy phone anyway and you get it back after class." We had many laughs about it but I also spoke to them about the power of having a voice and how if they feel strongly about something, they should pursue it.

Some may view this as giving students too much power, but I saw it as an opportunity to work together and satisfy everyone involved. When you include students in their educational environment, they take ownership toward lifelong learning.

SECRET 3: INCLUDE ME/AM I INCLUDED?

"Tell Me and I Forget; Teach Me and I May Remember; Involve Me and I Learn."

-Benjamin Franklin

VOLUNTOLD WHAT TO DO

The third secret in **"7 Secrets for Beating Educator Burnout"** is making sure that people feel included. When people feel like they are in an *inclusive* atmosphere, they are better able to contribute to the group and their society without fear of being ostracized. By bringing their ideas forward, they are offering a unique perspective, which typically stems from their lived experiences.

Am I included? Is everyone in the classroom included? As teachers, are your thoughts and perspectives included? When the system of education begins to reshape its approach to collaborative growth, the outcomes will connect with the 21st-century skill of collaboration that is needed on a global scale. Some examples of inclusive collaborative efforts are:

- **Enhanced Student Engagement and Ownership:** When scholars have a say in decisions that affect their education, they feel more engaged and invested in their learning journey. By actively involving scholars in decision-making processes, schools foster a sense of ownership and responsibility among scholars, leading to increased motivation and participation in academic and extracurricular activities.

- **Improved Learning Environment:** Scholars are the ones directly experiencing the learning environment on a daily basis. Their insights into what works and what doesn't can provide invaluable feedback for improving teaching methods, curriculum design, and school policies. By listening to scholar perspectives, educators and administrators can create a more supportive, inclusive, and conducive learning environment that meets the diverse needs of all learners.

- **Promotion of Equity and Inclusion:** Every scholar brings a unique set of experiences, perspectives, and needs to the classroom. By incorporating scholar voices into decision-making processes, schools can better understand and address the diverse challenges and barriers that scholars face. This promotes equity and inclusion by ensuring that the voices of marginalized or underrepresented scholar populations are heard and valued in shaping policies and practices that affect their educational experiences.

- **Professional Development and Collaboration:** Teachers are on the front lines of education and possess valuable insights into the effectiveness of instructional strategies, curriculum alignment, and classroom management techniques. By actively involving teachers in decision-making processes, schools can leverage their expertise to improve teaching and learning outcomes. Furthermore, fostering a culture of collaboration and shared decision-making among educators promotes professional development and creates opportunities for peer learning and support.

- **Strengthened School Community and Culture:** Inclusive decision-making processes that incorporate both scholar and teacher voices contribute to the development of a strong and cohesive school community. By fostering open communication, trust, and mutual respect among all stakeholders, schools can cultivate a positive and supportive culture where everyone feels valued and empowered to contribute to the collective goals of academic excellence and scholar success.

Scholars are thinking about inclusion as they make sense of the world around them. *Teachers* are professionals but they still want to ensure they are included within the overall landscape of the lives they are attempting to change. If you don't think so, visit a *teachers' lounge* and listen to their complaints and frustration. This can and will be challenging to *school district* leaders and administrators but without challenges what growth is realistically taking place?

I (VOLUN)TOLD YOU WHAT TO DO.

Let's look at an example of a common occurrence during the school day where a teacher is told to drop all of their plans and shift into something that the district needs done. The school administrators make PA announcements to communicate a message from the Central Office to drop everything and complete a specific task that must be done without delay. Teachers may feel like the identified task or project isn't extremely important at the current moment or they likely had their own specific tasks to accomplish that day. However, everything has instantly changed according to the district powers that be. Scholars notice their teachers' frustrations and recognize how even teachers are *voiceless* at times. But, these quick unplanned changes regularly happen to scholars throughout their school day. Imagine the possibilities of *inclusive* culture from the district level down to the classrooms. This may seem far-fetched but it happens in many real world situations and institutions. As a classroom leader, you have the power to help scholars see this way of thinking as a real possibility.

Inclusivity can look a lot of different ways. Make it a point to model and speak to an *inclusive* setting for your scholars. During the educational process many scholars don't feel included which can lead to being emotionally and mentally uninvested. If scholars are not invested, they aren't going to be giving my maximum effort. If scholars aren't giving maximum effort, what are they doing? Are they causing behavioral issues? Are they distracting other scholars? Are they distracting the teacher? Are they distracting themselves? Effective Classroom management should include lots of reflection questions to help with teacher growth. It is important as a teacher that you know your audience and the scholars that are represented in your classroom. It is wise to ask yourself as you're planning your *inclusive* lessons and activities how can you best appeal to your audience? What does my audience look like? What does my audience think about certain topics? What are their family and community values? Where do they come from? Where do their families come from? All of these types of things are important. When do teachers have time to cover these questions?

Traditional teaching tells us that this should be done at the beginning of the school year. The reality is that this should be done at the start of the year and then sustained through the entire year. There's constantly new information provided by scholars and your daily experiences with them will allow the relationship to grow. With this book we are ending the myth that relationship building happens during the first week or two of school. As an adult you have had different friendships for quite some time, you have friends who were your friends back in elementary school, and maybe you kept in touch with them through middle school and up to high school. You've had years and years to cultivate and work on those relationships. Why would it be any different in a classroom? The truth of the matter is, that it is not different, and you have to allow scholars to be *included* while having less time to include them.

INCLUSIVE CURRICULUM

There has been plenty of research about the adult learning model that states adults want to learn about things they have an interest in. Why would this theory only apply to *adult learners*? This is clearly applicable to *scholars* as well and is something that education hasn't addressed collectively for over 100 years. Think about the lives of your scholars. When you intentionally include scholars every day, you will learn details about them. Don't lean on assumptions! Be strategic about talking to your scholars. Talk about their lives and figure out how you're going to include your findings in your lessons. It is also non-negotiable to be very transparent and realistic; scholars respect adults that keep it real. Make it a point to let them understand that there are going to be days and lessons where the information being covered is *NOT* going to include their voice, but in order to make connections and give you background knowledge, we have to cover some of the boring stuff. Scholars respect transparency.

For example, you may be covering a specific history lesson that helps set the foundation of transitioning to the present time. From your perspective, you can relate to how the scholars may find it boring; however, the reality of many situations is we must be exposed to information we think is boring or irrelevant. When you are comfortable letting scholars know upfront what is coming, they will respect your transparency. Sharing your honest opinion about the curriculum and how you plan to use it to bring focus to a specific *scholar-centered* topic will guarantee connection and allow your scholars to feel included.

As the *classroom leader* it is on *you* to set the foundation of inclusivity for your classroom space, there needs to be an expectation that you plan for scholars to *teach you*. This should go beyond just verbally telling them and it is not limited to *academic learning*. Imagine the shift for scholars knowing that they're coming to your classroom to learn while also expecting to teach you things from their lens regardless if mainstream society sees it as valuable. Remember to give kids feelings that they will never forget. Scholars will learn things through your actions, reactions, body language, and your tone. You will have many opportunities to allow your scholars to be experts of their own experiences and teach you if you allow them to genuinely be included. When they are teaching you things and they see that you are actively engaged in the information they are displaying, more barriers are being broken. Unfortunately, many teachers claim to promote this type of educational setting, but their actions show otherwise. Being intentional with this will allow your scholars to now feel included.

Don't try to limit what you think should be included or excluded in what they are teaching you without having conversations with your scholars. An often-overlooked key component of teaching in today's society is a level of responsibility to learn the truth about the community you serve, their truth. You are letting them know that you are trusting them to teach you the truth about their generational norms and their truth will help shape your truth. The schoolteacher demographics for *urban school districts* prove that the likelihood of having teachers that live in the community is nearly impossible. One layer of hope will go a long way with changing the mentality. This is a reality that should be recognized and discussed more often not to demean but to promote diverse conversations. This practice will help scholars and teachers grasp the notion of developing trust in the person delivering the information. Scholars are masters of their own experiences regardless of their age. Age doesn't tell us how many lived experiences a person has had. A 16-year-old young person could have the same amount of living experiences as a 32-year-old adult. It is wise for teachers not to get so caught up in chronological age when thinking of *scholar expertise* that they forget scholars are dealing with life outside of the school building, especially in today's Social Media comparison world. When scholars are dealing with life outside of the building, we must consider how we're going to go about letting them express themselves to us. The reality is that our current scholars don't just deal with problems in school because people have access to them 24 hours a day. This brings *mental health* concerns that we will never be able to relate to because this wasn't part of our development so what better opportunity than to learn from the experts. Teaching today requires you to wear multiple hats, figuring out the balance that works for your classroom will do wonders for your mental health. Only you can control your mental health!

INCLUDE MY LEARNING STYLE?

"If a child can't learn the way we teach, maybe we should teach the way they learn" Ignacio Estrada. Research tells us that there are 4 learning styles: visual, auditory, read and write and kinesthetic (Shah, 2013). *15 years of practical experience* showed me that *multiple learning styles aren't always welcomed* in the space of education, especially when a teacher is used to delivering instruction just one way (*Lecture sighhhhhhhh*). Think about the classrooms that currently only use lecture style delivery in 2024 as the primary way to communicate their information. Tik Tok, one of the most used Social Media sites for people, is looking to capture your attention in less than 30 seconds! Imagine the discipline problems teaching with the majority lecture style creates because the educational traditional way to deliver information is to "sit and get" the important information. Obviously, there is a time and a place for lecture style instruction but it is imperative that we adjust with scholars' learning styles and the current times. By choosing only lecture style there becomes the reality that multiple learning styles aren't being taken into consideration. It is very, very important that we consider this information when it's time for us to find out if everyone is included. How many learning styles do you incorporate in your planning? How many ways do you allow scholars to show mastery of the information that you were providing them? Are they able to reteach it? Retell it? These things are very important ways to show mastery. There is the reality that teachers teach the same way that they were socialized. Learning institutions are still adjusting to accepting learning that comes from sources other than lecture. Think about how the majority of information is currently delivered on college campuses. As we continue to see innovation and change in our world the teacher prep programs will have to look at the opportunity to have a trickle-down effect into our new teachers.

INCLUSIVE GROUPS

An additional factor to consider with *scholar learning style* is how you can group scholars while you are including them in your planning. When you're grouping scholars, you can group by *similarities, differences*, reading levels, academic levels, and you can be very creative with your choice of grouping. You can even *randomly select* scholars to work together so that you're mixing your groups and scholars are learning with and about their peers. You also should allow your scholars' opportunities to select their groups, providing them with a chance to lead can help the classroom culture because they are included in the daily functions. As they learn more about one another, they will become more comfortable. As they become more comfortable, your classroom environment changes and you're able to manage your classroom strategically. This is assuming that you will be creative in how you deliver instruction, using methods like *Project Based Learning* (PBL) and other *collaborative thinking methods*. Creative methods help eliminate the unplanned opportunity to be a distraction in your classroom. Remember, failure is a great teaching tool.

CONSTANT ACCESS TO INFORMATION

Allen Klein stated "The ability to draw and communicate visually can no longer be seen as optional". Generation Z scholars have lived with access to the internet at their fingertips their entire lives. If I always have access to the internet, that means I'm able to constantly watch videos. Constantly watching videos means that people are always getting new information. It doesn't necessarily mean that all of this new information is true. It does mean that people always have access to it and are able to decipher and make decisions on whether this information is something they need and allow it to help them progress throughout the day. Helping scholars decipher credible information is more beneficial than just *telling* them that it isn't. Showing scholars that you appreciate their efforts to learn independently is a form of empowerment that you can now help guide. These ways of including them allow for a more scholar-centered space. The greatest thing about this technological era is that scholars can teach you so much about their way of life, allowing them to tell you about their expertise. You must have an open mind! Imagine the confidence they feel expressing their creativity. Allow your scholars to write about things, make videos, create songs, act out skits, and explore any other *creative* forms of expression they desire. Adopting these tactics will help ensure that your classroom is inclusive and welcomes multiple learning styles.

EVERYDAY STARS

When reflecting on my experiences as a classroom teacher and considering my observant nature, I often noticed many things during class changes. Teaching in a high school, I observed that most athletes had some form of connection with one another. Whether it was the girls on the basketball team or the boys on the track team, each athlete had a sense of community that shaped their school experience. School can evoke various feelings in scholars—anxiety, excitement, stress, and overwhelm, among others. Parents and adults place expectations on them, adding to the pressure.

As a classroom teacher or school leader, how can you create an inclusive environment that helps scholars alleviate these negative feelings from everyday life? When I ask this question, I think about scholars like the average "Derrick or Kisha". They aren't involved in activities, aren't very social, and dislike large groups or crowds. Every day, they navigate an environment that triggers these unwanted feelings and might go unnoticed by their peers or adults.

Simply being a positive presence in the hallway and taking the small step of greeting scholars you don't teach can make a difference. Including scholars doesn't require developing deep relationships with each one; it means humanizing as many as possible. In the classroom, scholars who aren't high achievers or who show behavioral concerns might never feel fully integrated into the school community.

I understand that teachers have a daunting task in meeting all scholars' needs, so creating an inclusive space is essential. When scholars can identify similarities with others, they feel a strong sense of belonging. In education today, moments like these are increasingly crucial to scholars' overall well-being and are within our control.

REFLECTION QUESTIONS:

- Have I created lesson plans that include scholar voice?
- Do I conduct curriculum audits to ensure an inclusive perspective is represented? How can I use real-life situations to make connections to my scholars' lives?
- In what ways can I incorporate various approaches to presenting new information to ensure I'm connecting with the diverse scholar needs in my classroom?
- Do I regularly hold classroom meetings to discuss my scholars' feelings and allow them to express themselves?
- As a teacher how do I feel when administrators don't include me in decisions that impact my daily activities? Do I ensure that my classroom is a model of what I would like to see?

DATA DIVE

TEACHING IN THE TRENCHES

Data will always be a key piece in the world of education. In my opinion, it is time that we analyze the way that we collect data because using only quantitative measures doesn't tell the full story. I think about the time schools returned to in-person teaching after the COVID-19 lockdown. Educators, students, and families experienced some challenges that were very unfamiliar and unexpected. While I was teaching during lockdown, there was one particular student who was struggling. Although everyone was struggling in their own way, this student received extra negative attention from some of my colleagues.

Before the pandemic, he had been struggling academically with in-person instruction, but he was present every day. His standardized test scores were low, and he started receiving punitive consequences for making poor choices. I developed a personal relationship with this student that went beyond the walls of a school building. We had one-on-one conversations before and during the pandemic, and at times it didn't seem like he was registering any of the information. He was comfortable enough to tell me that his relationship with his father was toxic. His dad had been making promises to him for over a year, and "TJ" was tired of the lies. "TJ" said that since entering middle school, he really couldn't understand how his dad could keep making and breaking promises. This caused lots of confusion for "T.J." and he really didn't have much interest in school. This was one of many reasons that TJ was chosen to be in my Success Prep class.

In class, we did lots of self-reflection activities and group work. During instruction, I made it a priority to give scholars many chances to provide feedback about life, school, and many other aspects of life. I knew that there was power in allowing students to interview one another; I always wanted students to feel heard regardless of how we used the information. Interviews provide qualitative data and allow for a more in-depth understanding of the minds of our scholars.

There are other qualitative forms of data that can be beneficial to the climate and culture of student-teacher relationships, like observations, focus groups, journals, and projects, to name a few. "TJ" really enjoyed projects; he was a natural problem solver when it came to challenges in the community. He was very passionate about how young people could create change that the community needs. During class, we did a project about changes that could be adopted by schools to help scholars be more engaged. TJ's group wanted to focus on school lunches; they had many opinions about how the current school lunches were more of a liability than an asset to student development.

The scholars were challenged to research their topics and come up with suggestions (challenges and solutions) that we could present to the neighborhood Ward councilman and a school board member (both graduates of this particular institution). At the end of the project, the class conducted circles with their groups so that they could communicate the results to the panel. TJ wasn't listed as the lead presenter for his group, but when it came to presentation day, his group leader froze up during the presentation. Instead of sitting back and allowing his peer to fail, TJ stepped up and took over the presentation. He communicated their findings, explaining how they connected with lived experiences and why the solutions were simple from their perspective. The leadership skills that TJ displayed definitely wouldn't have been measured on the state report card, but they absolutely fall into the categories of a 21st-century learner.

I tell TJ's story because many times we have scholars who possess amazing skills and need help directing them in a positive way. The world of education really needs to analyze how we collect and analyze data so that our next generations of leaders can feel empowered about the gifts and talents that they possess.

SECRET 4:
THE POWER OF SCHOLAR CENTERED DATA

"All analytics models do well at what they are biased to look for" - Matthew Schneider

The fourth secret in **"7 Secrets for Beating Educator Burnout"** is using *scholar-centered data*. Scholar-centered data is a powerful tool in education that can significantly enhance the learning experience, making it more effective, personalized, and relevant to your *scholars' needs and goals*. One observation that I notice in education is that the emphasis on quantitative data vs. *multiple types of data* to help guide next steps. Data can be analyzed to find patterns and make decisions so it is important for educational professionals to consider what types of data can be used to inform next steps and necessary adjustments. As the world continues to evolve, the way that education looks should also evolve, which can mean finding various ways to obtain information about individual progress. For example, the trend that education has followed places heavy emphasis on standardized testing. Scholars take statewide standardized tests during the school year, get the results during the early summer, and then are released for summer vacation. While at one point of time this type of data collection may have serviced the needs of scholars to prepare them for life after their school experience, that currently is not the case. In order to prepare scholars to compete in a global market and meet the current demands, the role of education should shift to a more holistic data collection approach. By attempting to cater to your scholar's whole being it also requires teachers to have an open mind to different ways they can shift their delivery. By being willing to make shifts and adjustments teachers impact the whole child. That shift can look like adding the following data collections practices:

- Cultural relevance of *scholar's lives.*
- Real Time Feedback
- Holistic Understanding of scholars through *interviews*
- Personalized Education
- Empowerment of scholar *voice*
- Community and Relationship Building

As teachers look for ways to combat educational burnout, I believe that it is a mistake to expect the complete overhaul of a system that has been in place for many years. Instead, educational professionals' mental well-being would benefit more by enhancing the importance of transferable skills while still acknowledging the reality of high stakes testing will be around for the foreseeable future.

According to Merriam-Webster, data is defined as "factual information (such as measurements or statistics) used as a basis for reasoning, discussion, or calculation" (Merriam-Webster, n.d.).

DEFICIT DATA MINDSET

How does our perception of data impact the mindset toward our scholars? Is the data that you use to adjust your instruction *scholar-centered*? You should reflect on these questions often. School districts provide various forms of data, most of which may highlight failures and areas of opportunities for scholars. I think about my experiences during the first week of school during my time teaching before scholars came to the building. We would analyze the data provided by standardized tests; this data is a one-time snapshot of scholar abilities. Although it is intended to be a sum of capabilities that we use to inform our next steps, time has proven that many outside factors influence these results. In my building, we had low reading scores which would often suggest that scholars weren't capable of critical thinking. This narrative and delivery model had a direct impact on the teaching approach for many of my colleagues the upcoming year. This approach caused teachers to go directly into a *deficit mindset* to begin the school year.

I would always think of ways to capitalize on the fact that everyday living for many scholars involved critical thinking. It frustrated me mentally to think that grown professionals couldn't recognize this obvious factor. The thought process of waking up, navigating specific tasks to make it to school on time, helping siblings make it to school on time, and being strategic about their route to avoid certain obstacles were consistent daily realities for many scholars. As a teacher, I wanted to know how I could acknowledge and build on those strengths? How could I prove to them that they were naturally critical thinkers and could use that skill in multiple areas? It will always start with the mental approach because scholars who test low on standardized tests still can learn at a high level. Data is very important, but its interpretation and evaluation are critical. When these are done properly, educators can continuously empower their scholars and their own creative teaching practices.

Teachers should assess scholars in multiple ways to help scholars improve academically and socially. Data from surveys, interviews, scholar-led conferences, and even standard tests can be broken down into *scholar-centered* language. How can the data collection process used in schools evolve at the pace of the outside world?

Over time, educators have learned that standardized testing results that school districts receive during the summer months have not always been the most valuable tool for addressing the changing needs of scholars. When looking at access and opportunity research says scholars in urban areas don't always have access to the resources that they need during the summer months. Some of the resources that scholars in urban areas don't have consistent access to are,

- *Nutritious Meals*: Many scholars rely on school meals during the academic year, but access to nutritious meals can be limited during the summer months when school is not in session. This can lead to food insecurity for scholars from low-income families.

- *Structured Learning Opportunities*: Some scholars may lack access to structured learning opportunities during the summer, such as summer camps, enrichment programs, or tutoring services. Without these opportunities, scholars may experience learning loss or a lack of academic stimulation over the break.

- *Safe and Engaging Recreational Spaces*: Urban areas may have limited safe and engaging recreational spaces for children and teenagers to play and socialize during the summer. This can contribute to potential involvement in risky behaviors.

- *Access to Technology and Internet*: scholars from low-income families may lack access to technology devices (such as computers or tablets) and reliable internet connectivity at home. This can hinder their ability to complete summer assignments, engage in online learning activities, or access educational resources.

- *Mental Health Support*: Some scholars may lack access to mental health support services during the summer months, especially if they rely on school-based counselors or therapists. This can be particularly concerning given the increased stressors and isolation that some scholars may experience during the break.

How long will education keep using the current data collection system? When a scholar lacks these resources, they are less likely to sustain growth habits. This is how the "summer slide" data is determined. The "summer slide" refers to the phenomenon where scholars lose some of the academic achievements they gained during the previous school year over summer break. This is especially noticeable in reading and math. Why isn't the education system looking for alternative ways to enhance scholar learning habits that support the commonly used *mission* of helping scholars become lifelong learners? The answer to this question is long and people are undoubtedly comfortable going with business as usual. When you are working in your classroom, data collection should give you needed results in a time that allows you to make pivots and adjustments. If you can take data in multiple ways and make it *scholar-centered* you can provide multiple ways for scholars to show growth.

DESCRIPTIVE FEEDBACK

"We all need people who will give us feedback. That's how we improve."
- Bill Gates

Quantitative data is analyzed and broken down by numbers. We all may have heard the saying "men lie women lie but numbers don't," made famous by Billionaire Jay-Z. However, there are other factors that teachers can control that provide scholar-centered data and can change the mental trajectory of a scholar. In comparison to team sports, I want you to think about a basketball coach and a roster of 15 players. You may have never coached an athletic team in your life, but you can still comprehend that each player on the team brings different skills and talents. Many coaches who have found a way to consistently blend these talents have received Hall of Fame recognition. They were successful by adopting a multifaceted approach to collective success. We can translate this into our classrooms by paying attention to the descriptive feedback that we give to our scholars.

As a 6th-grade Language Arts teacher, you may have a few scholars who missed key writing foundation fundamentals that you were expecting them to have. This doesn't mean that they aren't able to grow and become better writers. This also doesn't mean that you are going to be the person who fixes the problem. Some teachers may mentally overwhelm themselves by thinking they have to solve every student issue. This is not possible. But you can use your time with the scholar to work on pointing out specific areas for incremental success and psychological growth. This will involve individual creativity at times, but how you approach guiding your scholars through this process can make or break your classroom experiences. Your feedback may highlight positive things that you have witnessed from the student's approach to writing. You can let them know that many scholars experience similar hardships. After praising them, you can specifically point out areas for improvement in their writing, for example lacking transitions and clarity. A possible outcome of this approach is the scholar will know that you recognized something they have been struggling with. Remember, scholars want to be seen. By giving specific feedback, you can provide specific examples and explanations to provide clarity and address possible anxiety. Sometimes teachers assume that their directions are clear and straight to the point or that scholars will automatically speak up if they don't understand the directions. It is extremely beneficial for your scholars to feel like your feedback is helpful to them as an individual. The best thing about giving descriptive feedback is the opportunity for the teacher and scholar to create actionable next steps together. The results of these steps can help teachers and scholars celebrate the beauty of lifelong learning.

CELEBRATE YOUR SCHOLARS' VICTORIES

Another component to consider using often in your classroom is *celebrations*. You need to celebrate, you need to celebrate, you need to celebrate, every victory! There is no such thing as a "small victory" when you are on a lifelong journey of learning, because every step is valuable in the process. Scholars are looking for validation from leadership to gain confidence when they report to school. Many scholars come to school with very little confidence, then while at school their confidence drops even more because it seems like they're never able to get things right. Whenever possible, your ratio of positive feedback vs corrective feedback should be heavier on the positive side.

Scholars can have multiple barriers they are trying to overcome, which can change day by day. Teachers must find data that allows scholars to adopt a growth mindset. Fixed mindset data highlights the extent to which scholars are lagging behind in their expected grade levels. This situation is in spite of all the efforts that teachers will make to try to catch them up. While this data plays a role in the academic preparation process, adopting such thinking can become a disadvantage for educators, due to impacting their mindset and approach to teaching. Educators should use careful analysis to avoid prejudging scholars' capabilities before they've even stepped foot in their classroom. This can result in educators failing to service scholars in the best possible way by viewing them as lacking skills and needing to be saved. You may feel the need to provide a solution instead of enhancing the gifts that they already have. Shifting your view of scholars as already having the necessary skills for success and focusing on unlocking them gives scholars the opportunity to go beyond external and self-imposed limitations.

THE CHICK-FIL-A MODEL

"No act of kindness, no matter how small, is ever wasted." Aesop

The need to prioritize positive versus constructive feedback can be easily overlooked. Think about the fast-food chain restaurant Chick-fil-A, which focuses on providing great customer service that is consistent across all its locations. Customers don't typically leave their establishment saying, "ah they were too nice to me!" Chick-fil-A takes the practice of giving positive reinforcement very seriously. They use positive reinforcement as a tool to intrigue their guests and encourage them to keep coming back. If you consider the feedback you give to scholars regarding data, it's an opportunity to make them want to return to your classroom the next day.

Educators are often accustomed to teaching and correcting errors, which can create a tendency to provide negative feedback. You may not purposefully intend to demean scholars, but if you are not mindful and reflective about the type of feedback you're providing, you might develop a laser focus on shortcomings instead of focusing on incremental improvement. As you continue to grow as an educator, focus on what your scholars bring to the table to help them gain confidence and improve their skill gaps. Use the Chick-fil-A customer service model as an example to emphasize the importance of how people feel after receiving a service.

THE PROCESS VS THE PRODUCT

As Dr. Jamila Dugan states in *Street Data*, "It can be easy to focus on where we hope to land and lose sight of the deliberate daily actions that constitute the process" (Dugan, 2021).

Let's start this section with a question: When you consistently witness a scholar's success in areas that aren't measured on the state report card, how do you approach this situation? Many scholars who command attention or attract followers are showcasing their natural ability to assume leadership roles in the classroom. As we examine education through a multifaceted lens, identifying data collection methods that reflect scholars' lived experiences becomes crucial for each student's growth. By focusing on issues directly related to scholars' lived experiences, you can create a creative platform to address skill deficits within your lesson plans.

A significant shift in approaching scholar growth and fostering creativity begins with embracing the learning process itself. Learning to walk requires immense resilience. A baby goes through stages of creeping, crawling, standing, pulling up, cruising, and finally walking. How can we adjust our thinking and encouragement processes to guide scholars in embracing their academic journey? There are multiple answers to this question, but I challenge you to leverage your daily sphere of influence to bring more attention to revitalizing this process. Start by referencing relevant, real-life examples that resonate with your scholars' lives.

ATTENDANCE AND PARTICIPATION

Attendance is a topic that is very near and dear to my heart, especially while working with scholars who are living in low socio-economic situations. I do not condone using status as a generalized tool; however, in my experiences, I've seen how a lack of appropriate basic needs and support for scholars and staff can significantly impact the academic experience. During my years as a high school teacher, I went out of my way to establish connections with every scholar whenever possible. I stopped scholars I didn't know in the hallway to check in on their well-being. I approached scholars and offered compliments and other words of encouragement as well. I would also joke around and have fun with scholars about attendance until one encounter with a female scholar. I had a solid relationship with her, and we would speak to one another in the hallway. I eventually noticed a prolonged pattern of this young lady arriving at school after the morning announcements. After witnessing a series of tardy arrivals, I used the relationship we had to make what I considered to be harmless jokes about it. This scholar perceived my comment as another devastating blow before she had even taken a single step into the classroom. One morning, while she was putting her belongings in her locker, I said, "Good morning, Alicia, I see you are late again!" In my mind, I didn't mean any harm, and since I had a relationship with this scholar and she had witnessed me having fun and joking with many of her peers about being tardy, I believed she would take my comment in stride. Well, that morning, she turned to face me, and I could see the devastation on her face. Her eyes were heavy and filled with tears, although none had fallen down her face yet. It was at that moment I realized that my joke was the tipping point for a young lady navigating extremely frustrating circumstances beyond her control. After I realized what had just happened, I asked if I could walk with her to class, and she agreed. During our walk, she completely changed my perspective on "playing around with my words." She said, "Mr. Smith, I really hate being late to school. But it's to the point now that I have to do everything in the morning. Not only do I have to get myself together, but I have two younger siblings that I have to help get ready and get to school on time. We don't have any family here, and my mom works twelve-hour shifts from 9 pm to 9 am." By the time she was finished telling me her story, she had tears all over her face. I got her some tissue and allowed her to get herself together. I then immediately apologized, and we talked about my intentions, but I also acknowledged that it was inexcusable on my part. One reason I had the ultimate respect from scholars is because of my willingness to admit my shortcomings. From that day forward, no matter what, when I saw a scholar come to school late, I offered encouraging words: "Great morning, glad you made it!" Of course, some scholars would be late and had everything in place for them to arrive on time. But my concern is to create an environment where scholars feel welcome. Some scholars are still intentionally tardy to class, but I challenge you to always self-reflect before reacting because we oftentimes have more control over a scholar's daily mindset than we give ourselves credit for.

As a teacher, it is very important to set clear and consistent expectations of what participation looks like in your classroom. Participation is another form of impact that you can control. There are no guarantees for success when it comes to requesting scholar participation, but your approach can encourage scholars who have repeatedly shown signs of disinterest or disengagement. A benefit of being a forward and up-front person is regularly having conversations with my colleagues about many things; one, in particular, was how to motivate scholars who don't ever seem interested in the work. I would often share with them that the key is to see beyond a scholar being disinterested in classwork; make consistent attempts to address the connection with the scholar, not only the content. I often use my personal experience of learning History during my time as a student. History was very boring to me, besides the random parts that would pique my interest. Approaching a disinterested scholar to learn more about how they feel regarding the curriculum and connecting it with parts of their everyday lives is part of what it means to work with a different set of cards. I wasn't interested in History because it was a one-sided view that barely included voices of people who look or have lived experiences like me. My History teachers that were able to pull maximum effort out of me were generally concerned about my well-being, and I could feel that it wasn't fake.

Let's examine something that will be relevant for many years due to the progression and advancement of the internet and social media. The bias and credibility standard is part of the Social Studies curriculum, and it is designed to determine whether scholars are able to differentiate between credible and non-credible sources. This is an important component of fact-checking because of the surplus of misinformation that is available online. If I only talk to scholars about the standard, based on the old academic content and ways of the world, without providing a way for them to connect and interpret it for themselves, then it's a gamble. Talking to scholars about credibility by referring to the information being posted on TikTok and other social media sites can be effective because it brings part of their culture into the classroom to garner interest. Of course, this can become time-consuming and challenging to accomplish with every scholar; that is why finding a way to include this as part of your classroom environment as a whole will allow you to target the one-on-one conversations that may be needed to push one of your scholars into owning their learning. The ultimate goal needs to shift to scholars owning their learning process vs. just getting them to do the work. During conversations with parents or guardians, you are able to discuss some of the strategies you are using to meet the scholars where they are. School counselors learn about scholar action data in their preparation for the field. In education, sometimes we become so outcome-focused that we forget about the different paths that can help us get to our desired outcomes. We are at the perfect time to shift scholars to embracing the process of learning, which should include multiple perspectives. For a long time, and in the majority of cases today, the educational story is not inclusive of all the people being served. The mindset shift to participation and its impact on data needs to change quickly.

REFLECTION QUESTIONS:

- Do you collect qualitative data and quantitative data on your scholars? Do you have data discussions with your scholars so they can better understand it?
- In what ways can you make your data collection more scholar centered?
- Have you ever helped your scholars break learning standards into their own language?
- How can you make celebrations a daily activity for your scholars?
- Are you quick to point out the negative when you give feedback?
- How do you think your scholars would react if they experienced customer service like Chick-Fil-A Provides on a daily basis?

BE CONSISTENT

TEACHING IN THE TRENCHES

During the week before school starts, all of the teachers gather for the opportunity to learn with one another. Training can either be extremely beneficial or a complete waste of time, depending on your approach to being a lifelong learner. Learning to work together effectively takes time, practice, and skill. Unfortunately, there isn't much opportunity to work with colleagues, or it may be that teacher preparation often involves going back to what we feel comfortable doing. Students pay close attention to instances when adults falter and lack consistency. Think about it: the academic culture typically celebrates those who are always right and condemns those that can't seem to figure it out. For the sake of this story, I will highlight my student, "James," who was a professional manipulator. He knew how to exploit inconsistencies to gain as many advantages as he could.

As many people know, once the morning bell rings, your schedule can be busy as New York City rush hour. Your day can be non-stop, and you have to be ready to pivot and adjust at any time. James had been in the self-contained unit since 4th grade. He was extremely smart and had witnessed inconsistency from many adult professionals during his younger years, and as a result, it was hard for James to trust. Also, his loved ones who often claimed to love him with words consistently let him down with actions. James and I were able to have thought-provoking conversations because life after high school is adulthood, and life is coming regardless of a person being ready or not. James would look for ways to twist the rules and expectations to meet his personal needs. He even had his mom send a doctor's note to the school personnel to gain permission to wear slides to school. Slides were against the dress code policy; however, some teachers enforced the policy and some didn't. My perspective is if students are at school and ready to learn, the dress code policy is minor. Schools have dress code policies that aren't very inclusive of multiple cultures. However, I am a firm believer in accountability, especially when you know what is expected of you. James would walk into our classroom with his slides, then change shoes in order to meet the expectations of our room. For classes outside of the self-contained unit, he would change back into his slides.

We started and ended the day with group meetings focused on Social Emotional Learning. During our meetings, James consistently brought up how the expectations in his 4th and 7th-period classes were very low; the teacher didn't really care, and he was able to do whatever he wanted. According to James, whenever an administrator walked in, the teacher would say, "James, you know you aren't supposed to have your hood on," or "James, slides aren't part of the dress code. We should tell Mr. Smith and Ms. Glover." We had already been informed of this by our students. Our colleagues had been instructed to hold students accountable per the school rules, but in all honesty, James informed us that this behavior applied to many of his teachers. In these two classes, students did whatever they wanted and had no respect for authority due to a lack of consistent accountability.

James continued, "Smith, these teachers be phony; they try to act like they doing something when the principal come in." James would often speak during family meetings about how other classes didn't have the same family vibe as our class. Our class was a nice blend of love and accountability, something that doesn't get a day off. James felt as if we cared more about him as a person than as a student. He told us that meeting high standards is easy when people know you care. Hearing all of this insight from a 16-year-old was a reminder to me that one of the best things you can be for students is consistent.

SECRET 5:
TEAMWORK MAKES THE
DREAM WORK

"If you want to go fast, go alone. If you want to go far, go together"

– African proverb

CLOSE THE DOOR. TEACHERS ISLAND

The fifth secret in **"7 Secrets for Beating Educator Burnout"** is teamwork. Collective Teacher Efficacy has been researched and proven as a strategy that can promote successful scholar achievement. Unfortunately, the typical day-to-day functioning of an education institution has given us the idea that individual teachers should be in their classrooms alone with the door shut. This provides limited to no access to the outside world. Surviving the school day involves adopting a mentality of "I can handle my class." As a teacher, when you begin working in a silo, it can be beneficial for your individual self-esteem, but typically it's not the best-case scenario for teacher and scholar growth. Typically, scholars have more than one teacher throughout the day in middle and high school. Even in elementary school, scholars have specials that they attend that are taught by different teachers. When a scholar has more than one teacher, they are navigating the space of going from classroom to classroom and interacting with multiple personalities. Scholars are expected to follow building norms and adapt to classroom expectations for each teacher. Oftentimes, expectations from their teachers are similar, but their style of negative and positive reinforcement can vary. Schools have building values while individual teachers have personal core values that they want their scholars to adhere to while in their classrooms. When this information is inconsistent across platforms, confusion on the scholar's part is a natural outcome. Not only is there confusion regarding the building and classroom expectations, but also the expectations scholars are bringing with them from their homes.

An example of the confusion goes something like this: A scholar gets to their 1st-period class and is allowed to listen to music in their headphones during class while they work. That same scholar then gets to 3rd period and is not able to listen to music at any time. During 5th period, scholars can listen to music as long as they finish their assignment regardless of the effort put into it. Now we have reached the 7th period, and the expectation is different from all of the other periods. The building norm is that no headphones are not to be seen during the school day. This is a reality that many of our scholars can face daily.

Think about the inconsistency that scholars are dealing with when the staff doesn't communicate and work together. There is the reality that our current system doesn't allow for much educator collaboration time, which must be addressed. However, as a teacher, how can you take the initiative to collaborate with your colleagues, support one another, and ultimately support the scholars that you serve? We constantly hear about how scholars today just "don't care about learning" as they are punished for "being disrespectful" when, in reality, there are many other factors in the equation.

When young people are dealing with inconsistent expectations and school policy reinforcement, they struggle to know what is truly expected of them. This is not to blame teachers; it is more directed at establishing the type of environment that school mission statements claim is needed for scholars to succeed in the 21st century. Scholars easily recognize that in 1st period, they can get away with tight-roping the school rules and then experience different forms of accountability throughout the day. Scholars are going to find ways to get away with lack of collaboration and structure every period, every day if they can. This is quite like a child who makes the same request of both parents at different times, looking to get the result they want. This isn't bad behavior on behalf of the scholars; it's the scholar reacting to a lack of structure in an age-appropriate way. It is also a sign of scholars taking advantage of adults who refuse to collaborate. Scholars are always going to test the waters to see what happens when adult expectations aren't consistently reinforced.

Now is the time to ask yourself, how can you examine expectations in your daily classroom routine? How can you compare your classroom routine and expectations to those of the school building? Having inconsistencies doesn't mean you have a school full of bad teachers; it just means that your building isn't intentional about everyone being on the same page. Different schools will have many reasons for allowing inconsistencies, but the focus area of beating burnout is to intentionally control what you can. When teacher prep does not focus on these important steps, it can lead to a thought process that includes just closing your door and surviving during each period. This type of thinking will absolutely lead to burnout because it is easy to become overwhelmed by trying to solve problems without the expertise and collaborative efforts of your colleagues. This problem can be addressed by common planning, meaning that teachers have the same planning time where they can work together, or intentional teacher check-ins. If your building doesn't have this built into the teaching schedule, how can you take it upon yourself to collaborate with a few of your colleagues? Team meetings should require collaboration along with strategies on being fair, firm, and consistent with scholars. These are things that we expect from our scholars, so let's eliminate the mindset of survival mode and embrace the 21st-century skill of collaboration.

THE CLOSE "MY" DOOR MENTALITY

During many Professional Development meetings before the school year began, many teachers would complain about having to attend. Common statements were "Why do we have to do this every year?" "Just let me go to my room and work alone," and "These training sessions are so stupid," etc. Coming from a realistic point of view, I understood some of the frustration because leadership would not always listen to the needs and opinions of their teachers. However, it is important for individuals to define which part of the PD process we could control so that our mentality wouldn't go straight to "I need to be by myself to prepare," but rather "I want my scholars to learn 21st century collaboration skills."

In today's society, having your classroom door closed can be a requirement due to a safety measure, however, that doesn't mean you have to eliminate collaborative efforts. When you have a closed-door *mentality*, all the training and strategies that you aren't familiar with potentially go out the window. This is because many people tend to enter survival mode and place more emphasis on trying to survive every 50-minute class session, which negatively impacts productivity. Here are some reasons why some teachers may avoid collaboration:

- **Excessive Training:** If they are in a district that provides excessive training, they are swimming in information. As a result, they don't want to *"look dumb"* by asking for clarity or assistance. However, when adults collaborate, they grow their expertise and scholars are less likely to succeed in manipulating the system. Teachers should be provided opportunities to showcase how often they collaborate and work together. A result from the collaborative efforts could be that they are more likely to reduce stress because there is no longer a need to figure it all out alone.
- **Time Constraints:** Teachers often have very busy schedules with lesson planning, grading, and extracurricular responsibilities. Collaboration requires additional time for meetings and

discussions, which can be hard to fit into an already packed timetable.

- **Fear of Judgment or Criticism:** Some teachers may feel apprehensive about sharing their ideas and practices due to fear of being judged or criticized by their peers. This fear can stem from a lack of confidence or past negative experiences with collaboration.

- **Lack of Administrative Support:** Without strong support from school administration, collaborative efforts can be challenging. If the school leadership does not prioritize or facilitate collaboration (e.g., by providing common planning time or professional development), teachers may feel unsupported in their efforts to work together.

- **Differences in Teaching Philosophies:** Teachers often have diverse beliefs and approaches to education. These differences can create conflicts or misunderstandings when trying to collaborate, leading some teachers to prefer working independently to avoid potential friction.

Addressing these issues involves creating a supportive environment where time for collaboration is allocated, a culture of trust and constructive feedback is fostered, administrative backing is evident, and diverse teaching philosophies are respected and integrated into collaborative efforts.

Collaboration allows you to adopt strong expectations into your classroom management style, which can be established with the scholars. Teachers can then share this information with one another and develop a universal plan to enforce norms and expectations. Think about times when you felt like your scholars weren't on the same page. This is an opportunity to collaborate and discover how educators can work together for the sake of the team. It is important to know that a team-first approach can breed resistance from colleagues who are comfortable doing what they feel is "working for them". However, being scholar-centered requires intentional collaboration.

I suggest having these conversations early and often with colleagues and putting the procedures in place before the school year begins to create a foundation for opportunity to collaborate. When teachers aren't comfortable with expressing or enforcing collaborative norms and expectations, it's obvious that collective teacher efficacy, also known as teamwork, is not a central theme. Be mindful of cooperating with your neighbor and being open to adopting some of their successful strategies into your classroom management system. This will help improve your experience with your scholars. Once again, if a child asks permission from their mother to do something and she says no, the child will often ask their father the same thing. The child is checking to see if the parents are on the same page and if they can manipulate the result.

To reduce teacher stress that leads to burnout, you must discuss individually *then* collectively what's working and what's not in your classroom management strategy. It's called "best practices" in education. That doesn't guarantee that all best practices that are being used will work for everyone, but it does provide the opportunity to take notes on how and why those practices are working for you or others. From there, the practices and suggestions can be tweaked to apply to individual classrooms. Simply put, the adults in the school building should always make it a priority to be on the same page. Collaboration is a vital 21st Century skill that schools *insist* our graduates must possess for success in their future career, social, and academic pursuits. Are scholars receiving demonstrations of this skill from their teachers and other adults in the building? You cannot control your colleagues but you can definitely control *your* approach.

CREATE A SCHOOL VILLAGE

When you go to staff meetings or grade-level meetings, and you are working together with colleagues, make it a point to focus on specific scholars and strategies that have brought you challenges. You never know which of your colleagues may have a deeper relationship with certain scholars or expertise that you haven't tried. Remember, the goal should always be to help scholars progress. Sometimes it may take a different teacher's approach to push a specific scholar's buttons and get them to respond, but one of your teammates has the formula. That is how *we* win (and stay sane).

One goal that educators should have is to *collectively* push scholars past their potential and what they think they're capable of achieving. Help your scholars believe that they're able to achieve their goals and demonstrate the power of being accountable with your actions. This must take place without displaying the great savior mentality, which is focusing on skills that a scholar does not have instead of what they do have. Your ego may create the mission of "I have to do everything" to save this child, but shifting to a belief that you must empower all of your scholars to grow the skills they have is far more powerful. Change the culture of your classroom by focusing on the types of behaviors and norms that are constantly being reinforced and evaluated. Be sure to seek collaborative opportunities with your peers; then, watch a classroom management *mindset* shift begin.

GROUP PRAISE AND RELATIONSHIP SUSTAINING

There are many benefits to implementing group praise and sustaining relationships in the school setting. As you develop the habits necessary to build relationships, what steps will you take to maintain them throughout the year? The immediate benefit of continuous group praise is cultivating a positive, supportive, and uplifting learning environment. The classroom becomes a place of comfort rather than one of severe doubt and uncertainty. Scholars will be more inclined to think about working together. Teamwork, a crucial 21st-century skill, will continue to increase in demand as young people rely heavily on social media and technology for their interactions, reinforcing individualism.

Creating this positive, scholar-centered environment sets the stage for effective positive reinforcement. Typically, you will observe a reduction in negative and disruptive behaviors when clear expectations are consistently modeled and reinforced. Your scholars can refine their soft skills, which are essential in a global economy, such as empathy, collaboration, and self regulation.

By committing to this environment, you not only help your scholars develop individually but also become an active listener who provides genuine feedback throughout the class. This fosters trust and engagement among scholars, allowing them the freedom to be *themselves* without fear of judgment. Thus, you can continue to cultivate *sustainable* scholar relationships.

Highlighting group achievements ensures that all scholars, regardless of their abilities or backgrounds, feel included and acknowledged. When scholars see that positive collective behavior leads to favorable outcomes, they are less likely to engage in disruptive behaviors.

REFLECTION QUESTIONS:

- Do I work collaboratively with any of my colleagues outside of mandated collaboration?
- Am I trying suggestions from colleagues that appear to be working for scholars in other classrooms?
- What ways can I intentionally seek peer teacher collaborative opportunities?
- Do I share successful practices for specific scholars with my colleagues?
- Are my building norms and expectations consistent across classrooms? If not, how can I advocate for change?
- How can the group praise become consistent in my classroom setting?

LET'S JUST SUSPEND
THE PROBLEM AWAY

TEACHING IN THE TRENCHES

"Fuck you and this stupid ass class." Imagine hearing this from a student when you're trying to help them achieve their goals and dreams. Before diving into Secret 6, let's discuss a former student, "Ed". Ed was placed in the self-contained unit in 5th grade due to significant personal challenges. His home life was turbulent; his mom struggled with alcohol, his dad's presence was inconsistent, and by 7th grade, Ed was the primary caregiver for his younger siblings. This environment fueled his anger and frustration.

Ed reminisced about happier times when his family was together, before everything turned upside down. His father's absence forced him into a premature role as the man of the house. By the time Ed arrived at school each day, he was already seething with anger. He felt misunderstood by school adults who only seemed to focus on enforcing rules rather than understanding his struggles. At just 10 and 11 years old, Ed learned he could physically dominate anyone who challenged him. He started getting into daily fights during recess, exacerbating his mismanaged anger.

The school decided a self-contained classroom was necessary, hoping it would help Ed, but it only intensified his anger. Seeking suspension became a pattern; one major infraction was leaving the room or school without permission. Despite having an IEP to address his behavior, these issues persisted into high school.

When Ed entered my school in 9th grade, I was tasked with helping him break these destructive patterns, keep him engaged in school, and ensure he earned enough credits to graduate. Rather than relying solely on his academic and behavioral records, I opted for a fresh approach: I wanted to meet and talk with him, understanding his perspective firsthand.

During his first week in my classroom, I asked Ed about his experiences in the self-contained unit and what led to his placement there. He candidly shared stories of fights at recess and intentionally leaving class to provoke consequences that allowed him to skip school without suspension counting against him.

Quickly recognizing his patterns, I began building a bond with Ed. We delved into discussions about anger management and how society often stereotypes black boys by their anger. When Ed attempted to leave my class as he had in middle school, I surprised him by calmly announcing over the radio to security and administration, "Ed has walked out of room 125 without permission. Please assist him in returning."

I could have taken the easy route, letting the principal handle it or issuing a referral, but I chose to handle it personally. Over time, Ed and I forged a strong connection. Although I don't have a Hollywood ending where Ed turns his life around and heads to college after graduating high school, he did make significant progress. His suspension rates decreased, and attendance improved in 9th and 10th grades.

Unfortunately, during the summer before 11th grade, Ed encountered legal trouble and never returned to my classroom. Suspending Ed would have been the convenient option, but many students seek suspension to avoid facing deeper issues. Ed didn't want to escape school or my class after we peeled back the layers.

Understanding the root of behaviors can be overwhelming, but it's essential. While consequences are necessary, positive relationships and a long-term approach to behavior replacement are equally vital.

SECRET 6:
THANKS FOR
SUSPENDING ME

"There are no problems, only solutions." —— John Lennon

The sixth secret in **"7 Secrets for Beating Educator Burnout"** is you can't suspend away the problem. According to Merriam-Webster, suspension is defined as "the temporary prevention of something from continuing or being in force or effect" (Merriam-Webster, n.d.).Suspension from school was introduced as a disciplinary tactic more than 60 years ago. I-AM not an educator that is *against* suspension but I-AM always looking at attempting to *change the behavior* that I do not agree with. One thing I have learned while working in education for a number of years is you will have scholars who are very challenging. The challenges will show up in many different phases, but ultimately you always have the power, based on how you decide to *react* to specific situations. You can have the perfect classroom management plan hung up for the entire class to see and you can all go over it every day. Yet somehow some of your scholars will still manage to miss the specific details to the plan. This is one of those things in education that can cause frustration and make teachers want to just disappear so that the problems are gone too. I use that analogy because many teachers have a belief that suspension is the answer to their scholars' behavioral issues when the reality is changing behavior proves to be much more complex. The ultimate purpose of suspension is to discourage scholars from repeating negative behaviors. From many conversations and observations suspension can do the exact opposite. "Research shows that when scholars are suspended, they feel rejected from the community, as if they are outcasts, and often their behavior becomes worse, which leads troubled scholars to find more trouble" (National Association of Secondary School Principals [NASSP], 2021).

During our morning meetings at the start of our day, scholars would become very verbally expressive in the middle of the year. Consistency had been established and after the scholars have felt you out for a few months, they've been able to feel that your love is genuine and the fruit of your hard work at the beginning is evident. Having guidelines in place doesn't prevent scholars from making mistakes. Demonstrating consistency and structure increases the chances that you will all be able to operate in a space that nurtures growth. Suspension policies derive from a zero tolerance methodology.

Zero tolerance policies assume that removing students who engage in disruptive behavior will deter others from disruption (Ewing, 2000).

Suspension, as a disciplinary measure, often fails to *change scholar behavior* for several reasons:

1. **Lack of Addressing Underlying Issues**: Suspension typically removes the scholar from the educational environment without addressing the underlying issues that contribute to the problematic behavior. Factors such as unmet academic needs, mental health issues, and socio-economic challenges often remain unaddressed, leading to a recurrence of the behavior once the scholar returns to school.

2. **Negative Impact on Student Engagement and Learning**: Suspended scholars miss out on valuable instructional time, which can lead to academic struggles and disengagement from school. This disconnection can exacerbate behavioral issues, creating a cycle of misbehavior and punishment without resolution.

In-school suspension (ISS), while intended to be a less disruptive alternative to out-of-school suspension, often fails to *change scholar behavior* for several reasons:

1. **Isolation without Intervention**: ISS typically involves isolating the scholar from their regular classroom environment and

placing them in a separate room for the duration of their suspension. While this removes the immediate problem from the classroom, it often does not involve any meaningful intervention or support to address the underlying issues contributing to the behavior. Without targeted interventions, such as counseling or behavioral therapy, the root causes of the behavior remain unaddressed, leading to repeated infractions.

2. **Negative Academic and Social Impact**: Scholars in ISS are often kept away from their regular academic instruction and social interactions. This can result in academic setbacks and increased feelings of alienation from the school community. When scholars fall behind academically or feel disconnected from their peers and teachers, their engagement and motivation to improve behavior can diminish, perpetuating the cycle of misbehavior.

CAN'T RESTORE WHAT NEVER EXISTED

Restorative Practices are techniques that are adopted by schools and systems in education to move away from a solely punitive discipline model. Restorative practices is a field within the social sciences that studies how to strengthen relationships between individuals as well as social connections within communities (International Institute for Restorative Practices [IIRP], n.d.). Two key phrases in that definition that stand out to me are *"strengthen relationships and social connections"*. The key to strengthening any relationship is establishing a natural relationship. Those relationships within a classroom can include scholar to teacher, adult to child, peer to peer. A teacher can ignorantly make comments like "I have a relationship with ALL of my scholars." As the *king* of scholar relationships for 15 years I even learned that I didn't have a connection with every scholar that I taught or interacted with. That never stopped me from intentionally trying to have an authentic connection with all of the scholars and it helped. The reality is some young people are experiencing so many inconsistent commitments from adults that they live with their guard up at all times. The truth of this situation is that you can only find out if you ask and even that isn't a 100% guarantee. As a person in charge of guiding young people and the decisions that they make it is imperative that you approach each day with a fresh start mentality. Simply put, that means that each day is truly a *new day*. A new day mentality is connected to the mindset needed when looking at flying above failure that was mentioned earlier in the book.

Scholars are paying very close attention to how we respond to certain situations and they will later use those experiences to navigate their space. During the 1980's and 90's, respect for adults looked a specific way. One thing that stands out with respect to today is the ability for young people to question and challenge things. I still personally connect with respect from the 80's and 90's era because there were many beneficial things that I learned about relationships during that time. Being an educator and watching the many shifts that have taken place over the decades, I choose to empathize with our young people to understand where they are coming from. I listen to my scholars a lot because their voice and perspective is extremely important. There has been lots of one sided misinformation pushed on scholars in the school setting. One major factor in relationship building is connected to the personal experiences that a person has had. With a general title of a teacher we may think of an adult that is in charge of helping young people gain necessary knowledge to advance throughout life. Teachers have been to college and have earned degrees to be considered experts in their field of study. Why wouldn't you want to listen to an expert? My experience has shown that the type of love and energy that a scholar feels from an adult changes perspectives . People are masters of their own experiences! Whether or not we agree with them is another issue but that is the truth. In many of our schools we have young people who are adults in their houses. *They wear the title of the person in charge!* Right or wrong, this is their reality. Teachers that acknowledge this reality will position themselves to develop a deeper scholar connection. I have gone to great lengths in terms of trying to develop a relationship with some of my scholars and it hasn't worked. I still held them accountable, had expectations of them, and made space for the connection to organically happen. One thing that cannot be forced is an *authentic connection*, but we can certainly nurture the proper environment for making the act of connecting more viable. Some young people have been let down by so many adults that it will take many therapy sessions and positive experiences for them to ever consider trusting others again. *You must* control what you can control. I know, deep in my heart, that teachers are real superheroes but we have to be realistic with the way relationships are constructed, especially when we are offering a space of true *joy*.

IF I DON'T KNOW THEN TEACH

When an educator is trying to teach a scholar something and it appears as if the scholar cannot grasp the concept, the only solution isn't to remove them from the learning environment. We must look for alternative ways to teach the concept. Information is learned when you can explain it and use it in a wide variety of situations. Your scholars will come from a diverse range of situations and are encouraged to handle things like conflict, learning obstacles and growing from setbacks in many ways.

People may not agree but the approach to managing undesirable behavior should be handled the same way. When a scholar doesn't know how to properly conduct themselves while in your classroom, I have found that ensuring that you have covered the things you have control over will help you with your mental health. For example, you will review classroom conduct expectations with the scholars every day for the first few months and as the year persists, you may lean away from reviewing them and use that time in a different way. It doesn't mean that the expectations are no longer valuable to you but you chose to somewhat drift away from that focus area. Young people enter and exit many different places where the rules and expectations vary, so it's always best to confirm what the expectations are.

I want you to think about how your staff meetings are run. Typically there is a set of expectations or norms that are covered at the beginning of each meeting. As the school year progresses more are added to the plate and areas of concern are prioritized. If that specific priority is not aligned with what some of the teachers would consider valuable they will likely check out mentally by checking emails on their computer, engaging with their cell phones, or displaying other behavior that shows that they are no longer engaged. I've even witnessed teachers outright ignore the norms that were shared at the beginning of a staff meeting because they are in attendance simply because of their contract requirement.

Staff meetings can definitely be frustrating and feel like a waste of time. However, as frustrating as it may be, it is important for you to control your mental energy as the group seeks to solve complex problems. Distractions are a part of daily life and educators should account for this known reality. This small change of thought will allow you to reference your role in helping move towards solutions vs complaining about issues without offering fresh ideas and perspectives.

REFLECTION QUESTIONS:

- As an educational professional what reflective practices do I use that will allow me to keep an open mind to suggestions?
- Do I understand that behaviors are communicators?
- What system do I use to have one-on-one dialogues with scholars?
- How can I use Restorative Practices to ensure that I-AM focusing on the behavior and not the child?
- What techniques do I use when a scholar isn't grasping the concepts presented?
- What do I do when a scholar isn't grasping the behavioral expectations?

YOU CAN'T GET RID OF ME

TEACHING IN THE TRENCHES

During my time as a behavior intervention specialist, I came across so many people who had never viewed my students as human beings. Teachers would make comments like, "I don't want your students in my class" and "you know I understand giving chances but your kids just aren't ready to be around the regular kids." These comments let me know their way of thinking. People who thought like this tended to have problems with kids in general.

My student "Darlene" undoubtedly had a strong personality. She had been through a very tough childhood and was forced to take on a mother role at a very young age as the primary care provider for her younger siblings. This lifestyle made Darlene hate other women because her mother was such a non-existent parent. Darlene really connected with me because I provided opportunities to vent whenever she needed to get something off her chest. I always let her know that, with boundaries (not inappropriately bashing other teachers), confiding in me was all good. She knew that if she tried to overstep those boundaries, I would simply tell her that "it wasn't a good time to discuss this matter because it isn't solution-based, when the time is right we can revisit the conversation." Darlene had natural mother instincts and her leadership skills were strong. One thing about young people is that many of them don't always know how to use their leadership skills in a positive manner.

Darlene was smart, but when she was taking classes outside of the self-contained unit, she had plenty of run-ins with other teachers. Honestly, a power struggle ensued because Darlene didn't like women, which were 85% of the population. Darlene constantly told teachers things like, "shut the fuck up telling me what to do" and "damn, why you always saying some shit to me?" Although Darlene was working to control this behavior it would resurface when she felt triggered. Typically, once an authentic relationship was established with her authority figure Darlene would no longer display these behaviors. Since she was very smart and actively working on improving her behavior, she eventually earned the right to receive her education in a traditional classroom setting. This meant she was in the general population for certain classes rather than just the self-contained unit. The problem was that some of her teachers would push her buttons in an attempt to get her out of their class. Getting her out of a class that she had the right to be in due to some classroom distractions didn't quite work like that. Darlene knew that she could receive consequences for her actions but she had big problems with teachers who didn't even try to establish some type of a personal connection with her. Often, Darlene would say, "Mr. Smith, these teachers think I'm bad for real, but they act like we aren't real people with feelings and they can just treat us however they want. The way my life is set up that shit is not going to roll my way." Darlene was successful in every class outside of the self-contained unit, except for one. This teacher had a reputation for picking battles with students. This was a shared perspective with staff and students because of the teacher wanting to control everything. It was a core class meaning it was required for graduation. A core class is Language Arts, Science, Math, and Social Studies. I tried to be as professional as I could by providing insight about Darlene's background to the teacher so that she would be able to promote a positive experience and working relationship for them. For whatever reason, this particular colleague felt like if she just wrote office referrals, the situation would be fixed. When the offense warranted suspension it would happen but Darlene just ended up right back in the same classroom.

During some of my conversations with my colleague I would advise her to have a one-on-one conversation with Darlene, but she refused. I let her know that we can't couldn't just suspend the problem away. The teacher told me that was the problem because "these kids just get away with everything" and that was the problem. At this point in the school year Darlene was only having issues in this class. Fortunately, Darlene survived the class and was able to graduate high school. She now helps young people with gaining leadership development skills and navigating brain trauma, something she felt she never received when she was younger. Many times in educational settings we look for consequences to fix problems students are experiencing, unfortunately research tells us that this isn't the only answer.

SECRET 7:
THEY ARE COMING
BACK TO CLASS. WHAT'S *MY*
RE ENTRY PROCEDURE?

"We can not solve our problems with the same level of thinking that created them." Albert Einstein

YOU PUT ME OUT. NOW WHAT?

The seventh secret in **"7 Secrets for Beating Educator Burnout"** is establishing your re-entry process. One thing that is a very common notion in the world of education is that when a teacher gets *extremely annoyed* with a scholar's negative presence, they will *put them out* of their classroom. There definitely are many reasons why this form of discipline takes place and as a former classroom teacher, I definitely experienced moments that pushed me to order scholars to leave my classroom. Sometimes scholars were distracting the learning environment purposefully and despite remaining calm and going through protocol, but a resolution could not be reached. Other times, the demands of the profession were taking their mental toll due to changing guidelines and protocols. That could make every infraction magnified, which can become bothersome and very frustrating. Or if there is no connection with a particular scholar and they have learned how to project their frustration because they don't want their peers to know about the educational struggles, that will show up if they try to participate in class.

Whatever the circumstances may be, the fact remains that a suspended scholar will eventually have to return to your classroom after enduring the consequence that is deemed appropriate from the principal. I want you to reflect on the thought process of the teacher and the scholar when it is time for the scholar to return to the classroom. Depending on the relationship and the details of the procedure, there will undoubtedly be feelings of uncertainty, curiosity, and anxiety on both ends once it is time for the scholar to return back to the classroom.

For example, we have a 5th grade scholar who is 10 years old and they are experiencing life changing events outside of school involving trusted adults . They may not be interested in connecting with any adults presently because they can't make sense of their personal situation. Their decision making abilities may be off, causing them to be asked to leave the room. They leave the room and are intercepted by the guidance counselor. A small check- in conversation helps redirect the thought process of the scholar and they are prepared to return to class. The scholar knows their behavior was inappropriate and is wondering what the temperature of the situation will be when they return. The teacher may still be upset (rightfully so) and feel like the 15 minute cool down conversation wasn't enough to address the behavior. The teacher will want to know what consequence was handed down. *A very important question to ask that connects with this scenario is what type of dialogue should take place between the scholar and the teacher?* Usually, a scholar gets their consequence from an administrator, the issue is rarely addressed between the scholar and the teacher and therefore gaining closure isn't a realistic outcome. However, closure is needed for both parties to move forward effectively. Acknowledging that the situation happened and developing a plan to move forward is necessary to establish solidarity. Closure doesn't guarantee conflict won't happen in the future but it's an agreement that can be referred back to whenever needed. One of the best ways to gain closure is through one-on-one dialogue that addresses the issue. These conversations don't guarantee that things will be perfect going forward, but it does help with the scholar to teacher connection.

Here are two options you have as a teacher once a scholar you've removed from your classroom returns. You can choose to welcome the scholar back to and start over with a clean slate. This gives you an opportunity to acknowledge that the punishment has been served and the scholar may be in a different mindframe. Or you can choose to immediately address the incident with the scholar because neither of you have been able to express your personal feelings toward the situation. Remember, difficult feelings can and will continue to exist if they are never addressed. I know that most adults assume that teachers are able to drop a situation, let it go, and move on, but that is not always the case. Teachers are human beings too, and their feelings are real and also need to be *acknowledged*. Some scholars may expect to be welcomed back to the space as if nothing ever happened. Having hard conversations with your scholars can be very challenging but beneficial to their overall development.

ADDRESSING THE SITUATION FACE-TO-FACE

Poor communication is the greatest source of interpersonal conflict. A one on one brief conversation can take your relationships with scholars a long way. There are always variables that can positively and negatively impact relationships and the most important is the ongoing personal relationship you have with that scholar. One on one conversations often have a different outcome when there is some type of bond to build on. It is important to find the best way to make having one on one conversations work in your classroom. Being completely transparent about your classroom rules and expectations will go a long way. It is important however to be as discreet as possible when addressing group or intense situations because scholars feed off of that peer energy. Removing as much of the audience as you can when addressing behaviors that don't align with the mission of the classroom is a way to create the opportunity for reflections.

FAMILY MEETING! CIRCLE UP!

"Family meeting" was a term that we used in the classroom that described prioritizing sitting together and figuring out how we could move forward with our instructional day. Every teacher can relate to feeling like not a soul wants to be there in your classroom or hear anything that you have to say.

The truth is, your *mindset* toward approaching this scenario can make or break your entire year. This happens to even the greatest teachers who have very effective classroom management skills. It is natural for scholars to be disengaged at times and wander away from the goals that are in place. Part of your job as a teacher is to recognize when it is happening and to be brave enough to pivot for the sake of preserving a healthy and thriving learning environment and saving time. Every family has periods where everyone fails to see eye to eye. That doesn't mean they're a dysfunctional family.

If you are an educator, you may have experienced the benefits of a circle conversation when attempting to connect with the scholar voice. Circle conversations can also help you learn how to facilitate meaningful dialogue that are inclusive of multiple perspectives. Every classroom space can benefit from having a feeling of a family that is free from judgment, free to love and a naturally nurturing environment. We have positive and negative situations in our biological and chosen families. We may have family members who we are very connected with, and family members who always remain distant. Through it all you try your best to remain connected with as many family members as possible.

Circle discussions allow you to have much needed communication with each other. During circle time there is no "leader", and everyone's voice is equal. Each can safely bring their vulnerability to the equation. The circle discussion is a structured dialogue that nurtures connections and empathy, while respecting the uniqueness of each person. During this discussion there is a strong possibility that some may experience a roller coaster of emotions. The circle can hold love, fear, joy, pain, hope, and desperation. A key factor of the circle that connects with scholar voice is letting scholars speak their truth while not feeling the need to hold back their feelings for anyone else. This can be done in a very respectful manner. Circle dialogue allows for challenging emotions and realities participants are facing to be brought forward with an ability to look at the possibility of change. The entire purpose of the circle is to explore multiple perspectives and for individual meaning. During circle time you may find very common ground or you may grow to understand why a person has very different perspectives.

Because of teacher preparation and the system of education, it isn't commonly celebrated to pivot into the space of doing what is best for the present moment. You may have a lesson that you are supposed to finish with specific deadlines and milestones to keep in mind, however if you are addressing behavioral concerns every 10 minutes, learning *will not* take place.

Scholar behaviors are communicators and incidents during circle discussions are no exception to the rule. When you first start out having circles scholars may not know how to react to or process the vulnerability that may take place. Some may choose not to participate or try to distract you from using it as a tool. This is another opportunity to create the norms and expectations for the circle so that there is shared accountability with scholars and the facilitator. It is important to keep in mind that you aren't creating an additional task, you are providing an opportunity for a deeper connection in your classroom. Think about the spike in behavioral concerns that we have seen since COVID-19 changed our world forever. Teachers may have kids who do what is asked of them every day, don't cause any issues, and are always ready to learn. This specific set of scholars may not get the recognition they deserve or the ability to have their voices heard. Incorporating circles into your regular routine gives you the ultimate chance to change this narrative. We are currently living in a Social Media type of bubble that screams LOOK AT ME and PLEASE LIKE ME! There aren't many better options for dialogue and human connection in a school setting other than getting in a circle and allowing it to naturally happen.

REFLECTION QUESTIONS:

- Do I have a process in place that goes through steps before putting a scholar out or do I typically just do it when I need to?
- Putting scholars out is a temporary solution to a larger problem. How am I considering the steps needed so that re-entry is good for myself *and* the scholar?
- During instructional time do I pivot away from a lesson that isn't working or do I try to strictly follow the pacing guide?
- What types of creative ways do I ensure that my scholars who are natural introverts have an opportunity to be recognized?
- Classroom conflict is inevitable. How do I constantly seek opportunities to learn new strategies that I can implement?
- What types of discussions can I have with my scholars that allows them to see me as a teacherthat isn't perfect and are willing to have dialogue about those imperfections?
- Do I think one on one conversations should occur before a child reenters the classroom when returning from a suspension?

WORDS OF ENLIGHTENMENT FROM COACH KENNY "JO-JO" SMITH

Whether you are new to education and about to begin your journey as an educational professional or an experienced teacher going back and analyzing your current practice, I want to leave you with a few pieces of wisdom to consider.

Scholar behavior can feel draining. Remember that behaviors are just ways that scholars communicate with us, sometimes in not so healthy ways such as (talking back, defiance, and interruptions) I encourage you to find your method of undressing the obvious symptoms and dig deeper.

Employee gossip is toxic. It is in your control to focus on being solution based.

We are heavy into the Social Media world. Scholars want likes and followers. Find a way to meet them where they are while upholding your boundaries and values. Every time you like or comment on their "content"- meaning assignments and classroom contributions (not their actual social media posts) they feel seen and acknowledged.

Your choice to work in the field of education makes you special. Allow your exceptionality to be life changing. Thank you for choosing education and I will see you in the trenches.

Much love and respect,

Kenneth "Coach Jo-Jo" Smith M. Ed

FEEDBACK FROM MY SCHOLARS

Feedback is always valuable and I encouraged my scholars to give me feedback on their time in Success Prep, a Social Emotional Learning (SEL) focused class. For the sake of authenticity , I didn't correct any of their grammatical errors of their honest reviews. Check them out and hopefully you'll be able to identify some trends.

*** Scholars who were chosen to attend this class were chosen by teachers, guidance counselors, low grades and numerous behavioral infractions from the previous year. ***

*** Per my teacher evaluation 86% of my scholars grew .75 on their GPA every grading period. ***

What did you like best about your Success Prep Class?

-I like that we can open up and be comfortable

-I like Success Prep because you can feel comfortable to express your feelings or if u need help with anything or feel sad.

-I can talk about problems.

-I like how open you can be and how much the teacher support us.

-I enjoy success prep because Mr. Smith is fun and cool, it was better when there were beanbag chairs and yoga balls. But other than that it's fun my classmates may try to disrupt but we didn't allow that. I did my work when asked. I think the class is very fun and entertaining.

-That I can be myself and talk about how i feel with no judgement.

-Its fun in here

-The vibe

-I liked how we talked about what was going on in our lives because other people had the same stuff. He helped us look at careers and make good decisions. Mr. Smith helped us be ourselves.

-Mr. Smith and the work that we did learning different ways

-We talked about good decisions and making positive choices because in Mr. Smith's class we always are comfortable with each other to express ourselves in a friendly way. What we did to get to be comfortable with each other was got to know each other. We talked about Self-Awareness a lot and having empathy with your peers.

-In this class you can be yourself and learn different things about yourself that you didn't know before. We talked about our reactions and our consequences. He holds us accountable for decisions we make. He talked about healthy relationships and having respect for other people.

-Mr. Smith let us speak our mind and say anything. We talked about what was going on in real life. We talked about college the decisions that come with it. We talked about self control and picking good over bad choices. This class helped me when I go through stuff outside of school.

-I liked that we talked about life stuff first and then school stuff the teacher was a great teacher.

-I think there should be more classes like Mr. Smith's class because I learned self awareness. For example when i'm sad or mad I can make myself aware of my feelings. Also self management when i'm not doing the right things I can see that and say I was wrong and I can get better. I also learned about responsible decision making like staying away from my friends that smoke or when they ask if I want to hit it make the right decision and say no.

-I like how success prep helped me outside of school and I can control my cursing more. I also can control my emotions better than I used to. I can trust Mr. Smith because we can have real talks and it stays in the group. He taught us about self awareness and self management.

-I liked that we could talk about anything and not get judged.

-What I liked best was being able to speak my mind.

-They should have a class like this everywhere because it helps with life decisions like making good choices. Not smoking weed and partying or going to college. We talked about not doing dumb stuff like not robbing a bank. We also learned about healthy relationships and social awareness so that we can be aware of our surroundings. We talked about the gang violence in our surroundings and how to stay away or not get involved in that stuff.

-I like that we talked about life.

-I liked talking about life

-I didn't really like it

-I liked that we talked about being adults and we not adults yet.

-I think when we worked together. I don't like working with people or the people I had to work with but I did it anyway.

-We talked about our lives

-Mr. Smith taught us about being ourselves and acting the same way even when our parents aren't around.

-I learned how to express myself and that is really challenging

-I liked the type of work we did with projects

-I like opening up and being comfortable

-I liked the vibe in the room and how calm Mr. Smith was. I liked when we were able to choose what we learned about.

What changes do you think should take place if you had Success Prep next year?

-Nothing is wrong with this class

-I think more students should in this class because it will be more enjoyable

-Nothing i like everything about it.

-Me getting my work done.

-Not presenting in front of the class

-More time outside the classroom

-Nothing honestly

-I think we should have free food to eat

-I don't think I would change anything

-I think all classes should have bean bag chairs

- I think we should have done more exploring

-put regular tables and chairs back in the class

-No changes to this class should happen

-People who don't want to do the work should just leave

-People who don't do their work should get replaced with other people

-I think we should have more activities outside of school

What did you dislike about Success Prep?

-Nun

-There is nothing wrong with this class

-I dislike when kids would be disrespectful to the teacher

-When people always had something to say

-Sometimes that class was musty

-The boring stuff we did sometimes

-*Some of my classmates but ian gone say no names.*

-*Nothing it was all relatable*

-*I don't dislike this class*

-*Nothing I like everything about this class*

-*Presenting*

-*Nothing*

-*Nothing to dislike*

-*I didn't have nothing to dislike*

What experience or activity will you remember the most?

-*When we can just be free stay are self*

-*Field Day*

-*I will remember how the teacher wanted to understand us*

-*When we game Mr. Smith the welcome back celebration*

-*Musical Chairs and games to start class off*

-*No real chairs we had beanbags*

-*Our deep conversations*

-*When we talked about who we trust and why*

-I will remember the projects that we did

-Our group talks and the way we were like a family

-Presenting

-I will remember the where i'm from project

-I'll remember where i'm from the most

-I will remember going to high school signing day the most

-Coming back to school after COVID

REFERENCES

Boston University. (n.d.). Project-based learning teaching guide. Center for Teaching & Learning. Retrieved from https://www.bu.edu/ctl/ctl_resource/project-based-learning-teaching-guide/

Ewing, C. P. (2000, January/February). Sensible zero tolerance protects students. Harvard Education Letter. Retrieved July 21, 2004, from http://www.edlettr.org/past/issues/2000-jf/zero.shtml

Glover, E. (2022). *Centering student voice: A guide for cultivating emotionally intelligent educators and culturally responsive classrooms.* Authentically Committed.

International Institute of Restorative Practices. (n.d.). Retrieved from https://www.iirp.edu/

Knowles, M. S., Holton, E. F., & Swanson, R. A. (2005). *The adult learner: The definitive classic in adult education and human resource development* (6th ed.). Elsevier.

Love, B. (2019). *We want to do more than just survive: Abolitionist teaching and the pursuit of educational freedom.* Beacon Press.

Merriam-Webster. (n.d.). Data. In *Merriam-Webster.com dictionary*. Retrieved from https://www.merriam-webster.com/dictionary/data

Merriam-Webster. (n.d.). Burnout. In *Merriam-Webster.com dictionary*. Retrieved from https://www.merriam-webster.com/dictionary/burnout

National Association of Secondary School Principals. (2021). Suspension is not the answer. *Principal Leadership, 22*. Retrieved from https://www.nassp.org/publication/principal-leadership/volume-22-2021-2022/principle-leadership-october-2021/suspension-is-not-the-answer/#:~

=The%20Research&text=Research%20shows%20that%20when%20students,students%20to%20find%20more%20trouble

Safir, S., & Dugan, J. (2021). *Street data: A next-generation model for equity, pedagogy, and school transformation* (1st ed.). Corwin.

Shah, K., Ahmed, J., Shenoy, N., & Srikant, N. (2013). How different are students and their learning styles? *International Journal of Research in Medical Sciences, 1*(1), 1-4.

ABOUT THE AUTHOR

Kenneth "Coach Jo-Jo" Smith M.Ed recognized his ability to lead people during his time as a student-athlete. Coach Jo-Jo was able to play basketball in high school, college and professionally which contributed to his leadership development.

Coach Jo-Jo is currently an adjunct professor at Kent State University in the college of education. He has educational experiences as a Bullying Prevention Specialist, Behavioral Intervention Specialist and Restorative Practices coordinator. In 2010 Coach Jo-Jo founded Ladies First Akron a non profit in Akron, Ohio dedicated to using athletics and academic experiences to improve the lives of inner city young ladies. In 2021 through his consulting company I-AM Possible Enterprise Coach Jo-Jo became a published author and currently travels to schools globally.

Today, Coach Jo-Jo is also a top presenter in schools across the world spreading the message of infinite possibilities. His message of a positive climate and culture being an action item resonates with people from all walks of life. His goal is to help scholars and adults realize the power of positivity that exists within everyone. Coach Jo-Jo is looking to create independent thinkers of all ages. In the summer of 2024 Coach Jo-Jo presented a workshop at the International Leaving to Learn Summit In Nairobi, Kenya. During the workshop he was able to collaborate with global leaders focusing on scholar centered learning.

Coach is currently raising 3 daughters with his wife Candace. In his spare time he likes to read, travel and exercise.

www.ingramcontent.com/pod-product-compliance
Lightning Source LLC
Chambersburg PA
CBHW082105140626
46553CB00018B/753